VEGAN DIET

101 Recipes for Weight Loss
Timothy Pyke

Table of Contents

Veganism

Veganism is both a diet and a lifestyle choice. It's about avoiding the consumption of animal and animal products in any way, shape or form. It has a lot in common with vegetarianism. Like that diet, it means no meat. Unlike that diet it also means no milk and no eggs. As for lifestyle veganism means not using or having any animal products in your clothes, accessories or house. So you wouldn't use leather, wool or any other animal-related products. Also, vegans don't use any pharmaceutical and cosmetic items that were tested on animals.

Yes, the implications of that are far reaching. To follow a vegan lifestyle, even if it's not all the way, is a life altering decision. There is no doubting that. Still, it has become clear over the last years that we cannot go on like this if we want to avoid leaving our children a legacy of devastation.

We've got to reduce our footprint. Veganism certainly does that. Studies reveal that a vegan diet uses only 60% of the carbon of the average American's diet. That drops to 45% in comparison to a meat lover's diet. Eighteen percent of the world-wide CO_2 emissions come from farming. So if everybody became vegan our world's CO_2 production would drop by an astounding 9%. And that's without driving, flying or shopping an inch less.

It is simply the ethical thing to do. What's more, as will be explained below, it is the better choice for your body as well.

Do Not Panic

Veganism sounds intimidating. It shouldn't. It isn't half as bad as it's made out to be.

First of all, it's nothing like you think it is. It is not a cult. It is not a group of ascetics that are trying to deprive themselves of all pleasure. Nor it is a bunch of new-age flagellants punishing themselves for the world's sins. Yes, some see it as a religion, but there are extremists in every group. At its core, veganism is nothing more than a lifestyle choice. It focuses on making us live respectfully and in harmony with the world and ourselves. Nothing more, nothing less.

And yes, in decades past being vegan was hard. It took a great deal of self-discipline as you were depriving yourself of a lot of textures and flavors. These days, as the recipes in this book demonstrate, it is a lot easier. Science and culinary experimentation have created many products that can replace animal products. There are numerous vegan products available in most western countries. Thankfully, companies have also taken to labeling in vegan-friendly manners. That certainly helps!

What's more, you don't have to go vegan all at once. Veganism isn't an on off switch. It's more of a journey. It is fine to come to it gradually, one meal at a time. If you want, start with trying to stick to it once or twice a week and scale up from there. Every so often you'll back slide. That's alright. As long as the road continues onward and upward, you have nothing to be ashamed of. After all, by embarking on this adventure you're already doing more than most.

How it Benefits You: Health Benefits of a Vegan Diet

There are five pounds of undigested red meat in the average American's gut.

The digestive system was not built for this and can't cope with this much meat. The meat actually begins to break down and decay. This causes the release of high amounts of nitrogen and other nasty chemical enzymes.

What's more, if this was all natural meat that would be one thing. But it isn't. Almost all meat we consume nowadays has been injected full of growth hormones, antibiotics and steroids. What's more, the fodder the slaughter animals eat is full of pesticides, which collect in their meat tissue. And when we eat meat, all these things collect in us, where they compromise our immune system and degrade our health.

Plant-based foods, in the meantime, are less complex and are thus easier for our bodies to digest. This means that we have a much easier time getting at the nutrition stored in these types of food. With these essential minerals, nutrients and enzymes in our system we end up healthier and happier. This we call the bioavailability of nutrients.

When we eat a plant-based diet, we strain our human grown hormones less, we end up with more stable sleep cycles, our immune systems become healthier and we recover quicker from exercise. That sounds pretty good, right?

10

What is so bad about Dairy Anyway?

One of the main reasons why many people move beyond dairy is because of the effects that it has on their bodies. You might have heard how dairy, because of the fat content, promotes weight gain and colds. That is far from the whole story, though. There is a high correlation between dairy consumption and health concerns.

For example, as milk is high in fats consuming them means we spend a high amount of our metabolic energy processing them. This leads to weight gain and means that that energy is not available for muscle building.

Also, as mentioned, modern farm animals consume large amounts of medicine, steroids and hormones. These also end up concentrated in the milk and dairy produced by those animals. Then when we consume that dairy they end up in us. There they have the same negative health impact as they do in the animal's meat.

And finally, milk proteins from other animals are not the same as those produced by a human mother. This leads to digestive track inflammation. You might have felt this. It's that bloated feeling you get after having had too much chocolate or milk-based desserts. Our human cells can actually rupture as a result of trying to digest these large cells.

And so, milk products have many negative health repercussions. They are therefore best avoided. Instead we should aim for protein sources more aligned with what our bodies need, such as nuts and seeds!

Vegan Shopping

If you want to live a vegan lifestyle it is important that you consider the ins and outs of it first. After all, if you don't know where to get vegan foodstuffs then how will you avoid animal-based products?

Therefore, the next time you visit your supermarket or mall, find out what vegan products are for sale. Usually, they will have a section with 'meat-free' or 'animal-friendly' products. And pay attention to cheaper, own-brand foods. Surprisingly, these are often made without using animal products!

Also, don't be fooled by those bogus words like 'natural' and 'diet'. These words have no legal definition and can thus be put on anything. One famous example from the 90s was the word 'light'. People bought it in droves, believing that it would help them diet. It turned out, however, that they were fatter and had more sugar in them than the regular kind. When the companies were taken to court they said, 'but they're lighter in color.' Pretty cynical but no less true for that. Two words that do have legal meaning are 'organic' in the US and 'bio' in Europe. So you can use these words to guide your purchasing habits.

Get used to checking ingredient lists. Also, have a smartphone handy so that you can google those words you don't know. To hide unhealthy ingredients from you, companies often make ingredient lists indecipherable. Don't let them fool you!

Make sure you visit your local fruit and vegetable market. These places offer wholesome, organic foods for a fraction of the price. What's more, many of the people you'll find here really understand and respect food. This means they can tell you a great deal about what's available locally and the might know some nutritious recipes for what they've got on sale.

Plan ahead. Many restaurants don't cater to vegans. This means you can't just nip down to the corner and get a bite to eat. So you'll need to prepare some things, like the delicious snacks we've suggested in our recipe, in advance. If you do that, then you won't find yourself in a (dare I say it?) pickle when you're hungry.

In fact, this has another benefit. Because you'll be taking most of your snacks with you and won't be buying them in the store, veganism isn't half as expensive as you thought it would be. After all, you can avoid all the mall bought foods, which take a big bite out of most people's budget.

The Vegan Diet

The idea of the vegan diet is straightforward. First off, it aims to reduce the pressure on your digestive system by choosing proteins and nutrient sources that are easy to digest. Second, it aims to promote a way of exercising that is more in line with how we used to move before this modern age. These two things together will give our bodies a large health boost. Note that we're not aiming at a particular form of exercising. You can do whatever you like, just as long as you vary it. Don't look to bulk yourself up and don't work only on muscle definition.

As for the diet, it isn't about you depriving yourself of calories or eating the same thing three times a week without fail. Instead it is about wholeness. Digestion, health, mind and mood are interlinked and all together determine your wellbeing. And so, this book seeks to address your body in its entirety. And we will try to give it exactly what it needs, while eliminating that which it doesn't.

The last time we truly lived a healthy lifestyle was during the Paleolithic period. Back then we ate naturally and exercised a lot (in fact, we were always on the move). But we didn't just do one type of exercise. Instead we engaged in many different forms. Sometimes we ran, sometimes we walked and sometimes we lifted heavy objects.

In fact, let me take a moment to warn you that only doing one form of exercise, especially to excess, can be harmful. For example, weight lifters often end up having a lot of heart-trouble later in life. This is because their constant muscle training wallops their heart and also makes their bodies too large for their hearts to handle.

The Vegan Diet seeks to give you easy foods that aren't too heavy on your stomach. This will enable you to move and take best advantage of the nutrients available. It also aims to make sure that those foods are organic, natural and as close to the Paleolithic diet as possible. After all, it was these foods that our bodies evolved to eat. So, no more modern processed foods, with the digestive difficulties they lead to and their high salt and sugar content. Let's get back to our roots and return to a time when we lived long, healthily and well.

The Meal Diary

Sounds pretty good, right? And of course right now you're bursting with energy. And that's fantastic! Mind you, we often are full of energy at the beginning of a new project. It's what happens after one, two or three months that matters. It's if we can manage to keep ourselves going that will separate the doers from the triers.

To that end, it is important that you don't start running before you can walk. Take things slowly and prepare. Start off by keeping a meal diary.

This is a tool to help you work out what you are eating currently (whether it be healthy or not). It will also let you chart your progress as you move along your journey to the vegan diet. It is useful, in that it will help you gather all that vital information you need, such as:

•   When are you like to eat comfort food? Is it at a specific time in the day, week or month? Is there a specific reason that causes you to choose to eat it? Are there ways to avoid it?
•   When are you at your most busy and when are you most likely to need snacks or readymade meals?
•   What meals can you exchange easily for other, healthier choices?
•   What is the moment in the day that you get physically tired? When do you need to find ways to boost your energy?
To make a meal diary you need a standard day-planners that you can carry with you. In it you write down every meal, snack and drink that you have during the day, along with the time you have it. You want to write down everything, from a cup of coffee to dinner and chocolate bars, in this little planner. The more information, the more useful it will be.
Also, note down how much you worked that day, how you felt and big occurrences, be they happy or sad. Then you can see how happenings and work habits affect your eating habits as well.

When you've done this for a few weeks you can start seeing patterns that otherwise would have completely escaped you. Do you consume more sugar if you've had sugar early in the morning? Are you more likely to eat junky foods later in the week when you've tired yourself out?

Also, if you're like most people, you'll probably notice that you're waiting too long to eat. You starve yourself, and then eat what's available, which is usually snacks and junk food. When you become aware of this you can do something about it. All you need to do is make sure that you've got healthy snacks available at those moments when hunger strikes. This will both make it possible for you to work longer and be healthier while you do it. That's a win in my book!

From Meal Diary to Diet Plan

Once you've been going for a few weeks with the meal diary you can start working on your diet plan. If everything goes well it will kind of naturally flow forth from the diary. Simply take your normal food choices and start looking at ways that you can replace one thing with another.

Start by looking at the recipes in this book. Many of those are vegan alternatives of non-vegan food and can thus simply be substituted. But don't let yourself be straightjacketed. Instead, see them as a jumping off platform. Let your imagination run wild. And yes, not everything will work out, but that's okay. After all not everything has to work and on the way to every breakthrough there are often a string of failures and semi-successes.

Remember to have fun with it! Boredom is always the enemy. This goes double when you're talking about food. So feel free to experiment, try new things and accept when something isn't working.

Of course, be sure that you put everything you try in your meal diary, so that you can find everything you've done in one place. Also, to help you improve and remember, start using a rating system. This shouldn't be based on just one rating. Instead it should have several different scales – one for taste, one for effort, one for practicality and one for veganism. Keep careful notes. It wasn't tasty? Write it down along with why so that next time you can do it differently. Was it good but too much effort for that day? Write it down then maybe you can try making it on a day you have more time. That way, your data will be more involved and more useful to you in a few months' time when you can't quite remember the meal itself.

Also, be aware of those days in the week when you're generally tired (as that's when you might end up ordering in). Those are probably not the days to be all experimental. Instead, prepare things beforehand so that you aren't tempted to grab the Chinese menu.

In fact preparedness is an important part of the vegan diet. Fortunately plant based foods don't spoil quickly. That makes preparing ahead of time quite easy. Many of the recipes in the rest of this book keep for a few days. Some even keep for a few weeks. In that way you can make sure on those days you do have time that you'll have something to eat on those days you don't.

If you follow this system, then slowly but certainly you'll substitute more and more and you'll find it easier and easier to stick to your diet. This will hold true even when you're three months into it. And that means you will be far less tempted to abandon this project. Now there's certainly something to be said for that. What's more, because you are writing everything down it will be easy to check your progress. That's important as that can serve as a great source of motivation. In fact in a few months' time, you'll probably be amazed and even slightly disgusted. I used to eat that, you'll think to yourself, as you leaf through those first few pages. And that, no doubt, will motivate you to press on.

A Final Note: Be unapologetically Vegan

When people become vegans, they often become apologists as well. As if what they're doing is an unfair burden on other people because they refuse to let animals be slaughtered for their personal enjoyment.

Don't even think about feeling that way. Being vegan is the right way to be. You've chosen to reject the mainstream way of thinking that one person can't make a difference. You've chosen not to be lazy. You're actively trying to make the world a better place. You are not a high-maintenance social outcast. Don't let yourself be marginalized.

While the rest of the world chooses to continue sticking their heads in the sand, you choose to do the right thing. That doesn't make you an outsider that makes you a leader. You are willing to do what others aren't to help save the planet, society and prevent animal cruelty. Remember that. And remember that when they ridicule you it is in fact them that look ridiculous. So why should you apologize? The rest of the world should apologize to you!

Be proud to be vegan.

And enjoy the recipes in this book.

101 Recipes

1. Marvelous Almond Milk

Let's start with a vital vegan recipe. This fantastically versatile drink is, to put it simply, the reason we can do without the 'normal' milk. It goes well with coffee and on its own and is chock full of vitamins. What's more, the meal that you've got left over at the end makes for great addition to muesli.

Preparation time: 10 minutes (4 hours soaking)
Cooking time: 5 Minutes
Serves: 1 liter

Nutrition Facts Per Serving	
Calories	29
Protein	1.1 g
Cholesterol	0 mg
Fat	2.5 g
Carbohydrates	1.1 g
Fiber	0.6 g
Sodium	0 mg

Ingredients

- Handful of raw almonds (unroasted, unsalted)
- Water for soaking

Directions

1. Put the almonds in a bowl and cover them in water, let them soak for at least 4 hours or overnight, then rinse them fully.
2. Put 2 pints of water and the almonds in the blender and blend for 2-5 minutes.
3. Pour the resulting liquid through a strainer. Put the milk in the fridge. It will last for about 3 days. After that it starts to taste sour.

Special Tip

- Don't throw away the leftover almond meal as you can use it in other meals, such as muesli, in smoothies and oat pancakes (see next recipe).

2. Awesome Oat Pancakes

Oat pancakes are a perfect example of something that you can do with the meal left-overs of the almond milk mentioned in the last recipe. What's more, it goes well with both savory and sweet, making it a great choice for both a meal and dessert. In other words, versatility and great taste, what more can you want?

Preparation time: 4 minutes
Cooking time: 10-15 minutes
Serves: 4

Nutrition Facts Per Serving	
Calories	122
Protein	3.3 g
Cholesterol	0 mg
Fat	5.9 g
Carbohydrates	14.9 g
Fiber	3 g
Sodium	43 mg

Ingredients

- Pinch of salt
- Oil for cooking
- 1 cup rolled oats
- 1 1/2 cups water
- 1 tablespoon oil
- 1 tablespoon chia seeds
- 1 tablespoon linseed

Directions

1. Take all the ingredients except for the oil, put them in a blender and let it run for 1 minute. Let the resulting mixture stand for 5 minutes so that the linseed and chia can thicken. (If it becomes too thick you can add a little bit of water. It should be thick and chunky, but not so thick it doesn't run off the spoon).
2. In a nonstick frying pan heat 1 teaspoon of oil. Next, put the batter in the pan, smooth it out and leave it to cook for 5-10 minutes (how long depends on the thickness of the batter). When the top of the batter is dry and the edges of the pancake lift easily, the pancake can be flipped. Give it another 5 minutes and it's done.

Special Tip

- You can serve the pancake with a wide range of topics. On the sweet side try strawberry, banana, tahini, papaya, coconut, chocolate or honey. On the savory side you can opt for tomato, miso paste, avocado, onion, mushroom, spinach, sundried tomatoes, salt and pepper, or anything else you can think of really. None of these ingredients have been included in the nutrient calculation.

3. Meal-in-a-Cup Vegan Fruit Smoothie

Fruit smoothies are simply awesome. They taste great, fulfill important nutritional needs and are fantastic as meals replacements when you don't have the time to sit down and do things properly. If the only reason the blender existed was to make smoothies, I'd still rate it as one of the top 10 inventions of the last few decades.

Preparation time: 5 minutes
Cooking time: 0 Minutes
Serves: 4

Nutrition Facts Per Serving	
Calories	229
Protein	3.9 g
Cholesterol	0 mg
Fat	18.5 g
Carbohydrates	35 g
Fiber	10.5 g
Sodium	10 mg

Ingredients

- Water
- 2 bananas
- 2 mangos
- 1 avocado
- 4 cardamom pods
- 1 cup shredded coconut
- 2 tablespoon chia seeds

Directions

1. Put everything in a blender, with enough water to submerge all of it. Hit the blend button, let it go for one minute and it's ready to be served.

4. Autumn Pumpkin-Orange Soup

Oh sweet pumpkin soup, thank you for existing, for you make dull days colorful – and I mean that in both sense. A well-made pumpkin soup is a pleasure to the eyes and the tongue. This is a great choice for those winter nights when the day's been dreary.

Preparation time: 10 minutes
Cooking time: 20 minutes
Serves: 4

Nutrition Facts Per Serving	
Calories	476
Protein	13.3 g
Cholesterol	0 mg
Fat	3.2 g
Carbohydrates	112 g
Fiber	34.3 g
Sodium	120 mg

Ingredients

- 1/2 large pumpkin
- 2 large carrots
- 2 sweet potatoes
- 1 onion
- 1/2 jalapeno
- 2 cloves garlic
- 1 cm ginger
- Juice of 1 orange
- Salt to taste

Directions

2. After you've chopped the onion, add olive oil to a medium nonstick skillet and sauté them for 2 minutes.
3. Chop up all the vegetables, put them in a medium size pot and cover them all with water. Let it come to a boil. Lower the heat till it is only simmering and then leave it for 20 minutes, until the vegetables have softened.
4. The onions and the vegetables all go into the blender. Let it run for 1 minute. Put the mixture back in the pot, add the salt and the juice. Let it come to a boil one more time, then remove it from the heat.
5. It is ready to be served.

5. Kudos Cabbage Salad

Some people claim they don't much like cabbage for its bitter taste. Those people have never tried this recipe. Here it's the combination of nuts and cabbage that turn this dish from poor-people food into something that not even your most 'sophisticated' friends will turn their nose up to.

Preparation time: 5 minutes
Cooking time: 5 Minutes
Serves: 4

Nutrition Facts Per Serving	
Calories	429
Protein	7.1 g
Cholesterol	0 mg
Fat	32 g
Carbohydrates	31.5 g
Fiber	6.6 g
Sodium	1551 mg

Ingredients

- 1 cabbage
- 2 tablespoons sesame seeds
- 1 tablespoon pine nuts
- 2 tablespoons sunflower seeds
- 1/2 cup malt vinegar
- 1/2 cup sunflower oil
- 1/4 cup unrefined sugar

- 6 tablespoons tamari (or gluten free soy sauce)

Directions

1. After you've chopped up the cabbage, put it in a medium sized bowl.
2. Warm up the vinegar, oil and sugar, in a small pot over a low heat. Wait for the sugar to melt then stir in the soy sauce.
3. Add this mixture to the cabbage.
4. In a pan, separately toast the toast the seeds in a medium heat. Don't do them together as they'll need different amounts of time in the pan. Throw the seeds in with the cabbage, mix everything together and it is ready to be served.

6. Creamy Tahini Dip

Some people think that in veganism you sacrifice your taste buds to your beliefs. This tahini dip proves them wrong. With it by your side you'll never again yearn for the cream cheeses, the French onion dips or whatever else you prodded with your celery stick. Who ever said you can't have your dip and eat it too?

Preparation time: 5 minutes
Cooking time: 0 minutes
Serves: 4

Nutrition Facts Per Serving	
Calories	93
Protein	2.6 g
Cholesterol	0 mg
Fat	8.1 g
Carbohydrates	4.4 g
Fiber	1.5 g
Sodium	58 mg

Ingredients

- Juice of half a lemon
- 1 garlic clove crushed
- Salt to taste
- Pinch of black pepper
- 1/4 cup tahini
- 1-2 cups water
- Fresh parsley, chopped (OPTIONAL)

(note that these ingredients may vary as you never know how the tahini will react – work by taste)

Directions

1. Put the tahini into a medium bowl, then add the salt, lemon juice, garlic and a few tablespoons of water. Stir the resulting mixture with a fork until the tahini thickens and stirring becomes difficult. Add a dash more water and continue. Keep doing this until the tahini becomes white and smooth. It is important not to add too much water as ultimately you want a dip-like consistency.
2. Sprinkle over top the black pepper and parsley and serve with pita bread if you want to go the traditional way, or try and other type of bread, crackers or fresh vegetables if that's not that important to you.

7. Fly Mushrooms and Green Stir Fry

If you want a wonderfully taste meal that you can prepare in under 15 minutes then this is your recipe. Add to that the fact that it's incredibly versatile, with it being possible to substitute one thing for another with surprising easy and you'll quickly find that you'll be eating this dish once a week – and you'll be looking forward to it every time.

Preparation time: 5 minutes
Cooking time: 10 Minutes
Serves: 4

Nutrition Facts Per Serving	
Calories	243
Protein	7.9 g
Cholesterol	0 mg
Fat	2.9 g
Carbohydrates	46.8 g
Fiber	3.1 g
Sodium	781 mg

Ingredients

- 250g fresh mushrooms
- 1 onion
- 1 cm ginger, finely chopped
- 1 red chili
- 1 red capsicum
- 1 carrot
- 1 bunch leafy greens

- Handful cashews, roasted
- Handful of chopped fresh coriander
- 2 cloves garlic, minced
- 1 cup rice
- 3 tablespoons tamari (or gluten free soy sauce)
- 2 teaspoons sesame oil
- Sesame seeds to garnish

Directions

1. Cook the rice. Stir it frequently to make sure it doesn't stick to the bottom of the pan.
2. Quarter the mushrooms, slice the onion into thin parts, and cut the capsicum, carrot and greens into strips.
3. Take a large wok or frying pan and heat the oil over high heat.
4. Sauté the onions, mushrooms, ginger, garlic, chili, capsicum and carrot until the onion just starts to turn opaque and the mushrooms soften. Don't forget to stir.
5. Proceed to add tamari and the leafy greens and give it 1 more minute, then take it from the heat, add the fresh coriander and cashews and toss it all.
6. Create a bed of rice and serve your vegetables over top and the sesame seed as garnish.

8. Scrumptious Fruit Dessert

Here's a great little number for when you want nutritional goodness and sensual flavor in one place. This is a great choice to round off a meal and cleanse the pallet. Note that you can use maple syrup instead of honey.

Preparation time: less than 5 minutes
Cooking time: 0 Minutes
Serves: 2

Nutrition Facts Per Serving	
Calories	218
Protein	3.8 g
Cholesterol	0 mg
Fat	8.5 g
Carbohydrates	36.8 g
Fiber	5.1 g
Sodium	25 mg

Ingredients

- 1 banana
- 1 cup papaya
- 2 tablespoons tahini
- 1 tablespoon honey
- Juice of 1/2 small lime
- 1/2 teaspoon vanilla (optional)
- Water

Directions

1. In a bowl combine the tahini and lime juice. Stir them together vigorously until a paste forms. Add 1 tablespoon of water at a time and continue stirring. The mixture is done when the tahini becomes creamy and white.
2. Add the vanilla and honey to the mixture, chop the banana and papaya into bite-size pieces and mix them in as well, making sure the sauce coats them completely.
3. Place the fruit tahini mixture into a bowl, add a sprig of mint and serve.

9. Cook-less "Cheese" Cake

Yes, that's right, Vegan Cheese Cake. It exists and it's surprisingly easy to make. What's more, tons of foodies from both side of the aisle have tried this one and none have been disappointed. The cheese here might be in quotation marks, but the flavor certainly is not.

Preparation time: 25 minutes
Cooking time: 0 Minutes (many hours in the refrigerator)
Serves: 2

Nutrition Facts Per Serving	
Calories	833
Protein	14.6 g
Cholesterol	0 mg
Fat	54.4 g
Carbohydrates	86.6 g
Fiber	9.6 g
Sodium	14 mg

Ingredients

- 1 cup pitted dates (soaked in warm water for 10 minutes then drained)
- 1 cup raw walnuts or almonds
- 1 1/2 cups raw cashews, quick soaked
- 1 large lemon, juiced (scant 1/4 cup)
- 1/3 cup coconut oil, melted
- 1/2 cup + 2 tablespoons full-fat coconut milk
- 1/2 cup agave nectar or maple syrup
- 2 Tablespoon of salted natural peanut butter (OPTIONAL)

- 1/4 cup wild blueberries (fresh or frozen) (OPTIONAL)
- 3 Tablespoons of bourbon caramel sauce (OPTIONAL)

  Note that none of the three optional choices have been included in the nutritional ` information

Directions

1. In a food processor, blend the dates, until the remainder forms a small ball, remove it and set it aside. Next, put the nuts into the processor and let the machine run until they've turned into meal.

2. Put the dates back into the processor and blend it some more, until a doughy mixture of both the nuts and the dates begins to form. It should stick together when you squeeze it. You might need to add a few more dates if the mixture is too dry, or almonds if it's too wet. You can also choose to add some salt.

3. Take a 12 slot muffin tray, lightly grease it and cut thin parchment tabs that you can use to pull the cheesecakes out. Don't have parchment? A butter knife will work as well. Obviously you don't put it in the mixture, you use it at the end to take the cups out.

4. Take a tablespoon of the mixture you've created and pack it down into the muffin shape with your fingers. Make sure it's really compacted. A spoon or the bottom of a glass can be helpful here. Set the mixture into the freezer to let it firm up.

5. Take the cashews, lemon juice, coconut oil, coconut milk and maple syrup and blend them in a mixer until it turns smooth. Use more lemon juice if it doesn't want to stick together.

6. If you're adding peanut butter, put it into the mixer with the other ingredients. If you're adding blueberry or caramel, wait and swirl it on top of the cheesecakes.

7. Take this mixture and divide it out over the muffin tin. Tap the tin to get rid of any air bubbles. Then put it back in the freezer and let it stand for another 4-6 hours and they've hardened.

10. Cool Chocolate Pie

The great thing about this dessert is that you can just make it one day in the week and enjoy it for many days after – that is, if you can padlock your freezer, because this beauty is so delicious that you might just find they've all been eaten while your back was turned.

Preparation time: 20 minutes
Cooking time: 5 minutes (several hours in the freezer)
Serves: 4

Nutrition Facts Per Serving	
Calories	947
Protein	26 g
Cholesterol	0 mg
Fat	60.1 g
Carbohydrates	89 g
Fiber	12 g
Sodium	97 mg

Ingredients

- 1 heaping (packed) cup pitted dates, soaked for 10 minutes in warm water and drained
- 12 ounces silken tofu, drained, patted dry
- 1 3/4 cups dairy-free semisweet chocolate chips
- 1 1/2 cups raw walnuts
- 1/2 cup light or full fat coconut milk (or another dairy-free milk)
- 1/3 cup unsweetened cocoa or cacao powder

Directions

1. Take a food processor, put inside the walnuts and cocoa powder and process them until it turns into a fine meal. Remove this mixture and set it aside.
2. Now the dates go into the processor. Turn it back on, until the dates have been turned into small bits and become a little bit sticky. Take the first mixture and add it back into the processor and process until it has been mixed together well.
3. All of this now goes into a glass pie pan that has been lightly oiled with coconut oil. You can also use cooking parchment to make it easy to remove. Put a plastic wrap cover over the crumbs and make sure that they are pressed over the whole pan, including up the sides. Then put it in the freezer.
4. Use either a double boiler or a microwave to melt the chocolate chips. Once it's been melted time is of the essence. Quickly combine in the tofu and coconut milk, put it in a blender and let it run for a minute.
5. Scrape everything out of the blender out and pour it over the crust that you put into the freezer a while back. Put it back in the freezer and let it stand a while longer.
6. This dish works surprisingly well with coconut whipped cream.

11. Best Cranberry Bread

The lovechild of fall would have to be this vegan cranberry bread, with its combination of cranberry, orange, ginger and walnuts. There is simply no better way to get the day started than to sample this beautiful mix of flavors.

Preparation time: 15 minutes
Cooking time: 1 hour
Serves: 8 (1 slice per person)

Nutrition Facts Per Serving	
Calories	370
Protein	6.2 g
Cholesterol	0 mg
Fat	11.4 g
Carbohydrates	61.9 g
Fiber	2.1 g
Sodium	280 mg

Ingredients

- 1 Flax Egg
- 2 cups all-purpose flour
- 1 cup orange juice
- 1 cup chopped fresh cranberries
- 1 cup confectioners' sugar
- 1/2 cup chopped walnuts
- 1/2 cup sugar
- 1/4 cup butter or vegan butter melted
- 1/4 cup brown sugar

- 1-2 Tablespoons cranberry juice
- 1 1/2 teaspoons baking powder
- 1 teaspoon ground ginger
- 1 teaspoon vanilla extract
- 1/2 teaspoon salt
- 1/2 teaspoon baking soda
- 3/4 teaspoon ground cinnamon
- as much orange zest as you want

Directions

1. Turn the oven to 350°F and let it preheat
2. Take a 9 X 5 loaf pan, spray it with oil and apply flower.
3. Combine the flour, salt, baking powder, baking soda, ground cinnamon and ginger in a medium bowl, with a whisk.
4. Take a large bowl, put into the butter and sugar and beat the mixture until it is smooth. Then stir in both the orange juice and the flax egg. Now slowly mix this together with the flour mixture until it is just moist, then add the walnuts and cranberries. Continue to stir throughout.
5. Pour the result into the pan prepared in step two and allow it to bake for 60 minutes, until the crust is golden brown and a toothpick comes out clean.
6. The optional cranberry glaze is very easy to make. Simply combine the cranberry juice with the sugar and whisking it until it's smooth. This then gets drizzled over top of the warm bred.

12. Precious Pumpkin Pie

What is better than pumpkin pie? A pumpkin pie that's low on effort, doesn't need an oven and still tastes like angels are doing a jig on your tongue. And this recipe does exactly that. All you need is a fridge, a stove and a 24 hour surveillance to keep away the crooks and the thieves.

Preparation time: 20 minutes
Cooking time: 15 minutes (needs several hours in the refrigerator)
Serves: 4

Nutrition Facts Per Serving	
Calories	1078
Protein	20.9 g
Cholesterol	0 mg
Fat	61 g
Carbohydrates	130.3 g
Fiber	17.8 g
Sodium	585 mg

Ingredients

- 1 13 1/2 ounce can full fat coconut milk (chilled overnight)
- 2 cups pitted dates
- 2 cups raw nuts like pecans or walnuts
- 1 2/3 cup unsweetened milk
- 1 cup pumpkin puree
- 1/3 cup sugar (raw or granulated)
- 1/4 cup gluten free oats (you can use unsweetened coconut flakes for a different flavor as well)

- 3 1/2 Tablespoon corn starch
- 2-5 Tablespoons powdered sugar, depending on preferred sweetness
- 1 teaspoon pumpkin pie spice (divided)
- 1/2 teaspoon vanilla extract
- 1/2 teaspoon pure vanilla extract
- pinch sea salt

Directions

1. First start by making the filling. Take the cornstarch, sugar, 1/2 a teaspoon of pumpkin pie spice, vanilla extract and sea salt and combine in them in a bowl with a whisk. Add the pumpkin puree, while continuing to stir all together, finally add the milk. Make sure it's mixed together well.
2. Put it in a pan and over a medium heat bring it to a bubble, though not a boil, while continuing to stir. Once it begins to bubble and thicken, reduce the heat and allow it to cook while stirring with a rubber spatula. You're looking for visible ribbons to form. It should jiggle slightly when you shake it.
3. Take the pan from the heat and add in the vanilla, while continuing to stir. Let it set for between 5 to 10 minutes, then put it into a glass bowl and cover it with plastic wrap. Note you actually want the film to touch the pudding! Otherwise you'll get an undesirable film.
4. Put the filling in the refrigerator and leave it for a few hours.
5. In the meantime you can make the crust. Put the dates into the food processor and pulse until they've been cut up fine enough to form a ball (if that doesn't happen, just having small bits is fine as well). Take it out of the machine, then put 1/2 a teaspoon of pumpkin pie spice, the nuts and the oats into the processor in its place and grind these until they're close to a meal. Now put the dates back in and blend well, until a dough forms.
6. This all gets put into a lightly greased baking dish that isn't too large. Press the substance into the bottom and up the sides, making sure there are no cracks or gaps. Cover this with plastic wrap as well and then put it into the fridge as well.
7. Next it's time to make the coconut whipped cream. Take the coconut milk can that you've left in the freezer overnight and without shaking it, take off the top and carefully scoop the top thick part of the liquid out. This is the cream you'll be using. The clear liquid at the bottom you won't need for this recipe.
8. Beat the cream, which should make it firm up; if it doesn't you can add a few tablespoons of tapioca powder, which will do the trick. Then add the powdered

sugar slowly, along with the vanilla extract. This also needs to be covered and left in the fridge for a while.

9. Take out the crust and the filling of the pie and pour the filling into the crust, then smooth it out. Now they go back into the fridge one more time for a couple of hours, or overnight if you've got the time.

10. When you are ready to serve, take it out, put on top the coconut cream and share it out. The pie will keep for several days if you keep it cooled.

13. Awesome Orange Scented Sweet Potato

Sweet potato and orange are like Bonnie and Clyde, a little risqué perhaps, but they go oh so well together and they, in fact, complete one another. A flavor feast that's low on calories, this one is fantastically quick to prepare and wonderfully nutritious to boot.

Preparation time: 5 minutes
Cooking time: 15 Minutes
Serves: 4-6

Nutrition Facts Per Serving	
Calories	49
Protein	0.3 g
Cholesterol	0 mg
Fat	0.8 g
Carbohydrates	10.8 g
Fiber	0 g
Sodium	75 mg

Ingredients

- 5 Tablespoon orange juice
- 2 1/2 Tablespoon maple syrup
- 1 teaspoon grated fresh ginger root Pinch of ground nutmeg
- 1/2 teaspoon grated orange rind
- 1/2 teaspoon grated lemon rind
- 1/8 teaspoon salt (or to taste)

- Lightly toasted, chopped pecans for garnish

Directions

1. Turn the oven to 350°F and let it preheat
2. The sweet potatoes need to be peeled and put in the food processor along with the remaining ingredients. Turn the processor on and wait for the ingredients to turn smooth.
3. Put the ingredients in a casserole dish until they dish has been heated through, which takes about 15 minutes. Garnish with the pecans and be sure to serve the dish hot.

14. Very Vegan Mushroom Gravy

This wonderful gravy can be eaten with mash, biscuits – heck it could almost be eaten on its own! It tastes good with store-bought "chicken" broth, but tastes even better if you're willing to make your own. You can choose to leave out the nutritional yeast if you so desire, but it does make the gravy that bit creamier.

Preparation time: 10 minutes
Cooking time: 15 minutes
Serves: 4

Nutrition Facts Per Serving	
Calories	214
Protein	11.9 g
Cholesterol	0 mg
Fat	12.7 g
Carbohydrates	17.3 g
Fiber	5.8 g
Sodium	446 mg

Ingredients

- 1/2 pound mushrooms
- 2 1/4 cup water
- 1/2 cup nutritional yeast flakes
- 1/4 cup white flour
- 1/4 cup vegan margarine
- 1 teaspoon Bouquet browning sauce
- 3/8 teaspoon onion powder
- 1/2 teaspoon salt

Directions

1. In a medium nonstick skillet over a medium to high heat, add the margarine and then sauté the mushrooms until browned and limp.
2. In a small saucepan, mix the yeast, salt, flour and onion powder, then blend in water to make a sauce, while whisking. Stir continuously as you put it on a low heat and allow it to thicken.
3. Cook it for another minute, add the mushrooms and continue to stir.
4. Give it the good ol' taste test and put in salt and onion powder if you're so inclined.

15. Crazy Carrot Muffins

Carrot muffins are oh so good and this recipe for them is great. Really, you'll be impressed with how they are not too sweet, moist and of so very, very good for you. The best of both worlds is possible and the recipe is called 'crazy carrot muffin'.

Preparation time: 15 minutes
Cooking time: 30 Minutes
Serves: 6 – 2 per person

Nutrition Facts Per Serving	
Calories	398
Protein	6.2 g
Cholesterol	0 mg
Fat	15.3 g
Carbohydrates	60.6 g
Fiber	3.9 g
Sodium	316 mg

Ingredients

- 1 cup whole-wheat flour
- 1 cup oats or wheat bran
- 1 cup raw carrots, grated
- 1 cup water
- 1/3 cup sugar or maple syrup
- 1/4 cup mild-flavored oil or vegan butter, melted
- 1 tablespoon cornstarch
- 2 teaspoons baking powder
- 1 teaspoon allspice

- 1/2 teaspoon ground cinnamon
- 1/2 teaspoon salt

Directions

1. Turn the oven to 375°F and allow it to preheat.
2. In the meantime, take a large mixing bowl and put into it the oats or bran, flour, cornstarch, baking powder, allspice, cinnamon, and salt and mix them together real well. Then put in the grated carrots, mix in the water as well as the sugar or maple syrup and the oil and mix gently.
3. Put the batter into a muffin pan that has been lightly oiled. You want each of the tins to be about two-thirds full. Let it bake for 25-30 minutes, or until an inserted toothpick comes out clean. Let it cool for 5 minutes before transferring to a baking rack. Let it cool some more and they are ready to be served.

16. Phenomenal Fluffy Pancakes

There really is only one drawback to these pancakes and that's that our family can never get enough of them. We just keep making them and making them. It's a good thing they're so straightforward! Add to that that they're adaptable and full of nutritional value and you realize that's a drawback you can live with.

Preparation time: 10 minutes
Cooking time: 5 minutes
Serves: 4

Nutrition Facts Per Serving	
Calories	322
Protein	9.8 g
Cholesterol	0 mg
Fat	10.4 g
Carbohydrates	48 g
Fiber	1.4 g
Sodium	223 mg

Ingredients

- 2 1/2 cups dairy-free milk
- 1 1/2 cups all-purpose flour
- 2 tablespoons vegetable oil
- 1 tablespoon baking powder
- 1 tablespoon sugar
- 1/4 teaspoon salt

Directions

1. Over a medium to high heat, heat a nonstick skillet until a drop of water immediately begins to sizzle when you put it on the cooking surface.
2. Combine the flour, baking powder, salt and sugar. When they are well mixed, add in the wet ingredients. You do not want to overmix. You can get rid of lumps by simply letting the batter stand for a minute. They'll break down by themselves.
3. Put a quarter-cup of batter and pour it into the skillet. Let it cook over a medium heat and flip them when the edges dry and the bubbles in the batter begin to pop.
4. Leave them to cook for another 2 minutes and then serve. You can have them with vegan butter, maple syrup, agave syrup or fresh fruit.

17. Savory Breakfast Sandwich

This wonderful sandwich is a round of flavors that will have all your taste buds tingling. With this dish you can prove to everybody that the vegan kitchen can do everything that the 'normal' kitchen can, while being healthier and more wholesome as well.

Preparation time: 20 minutes
Cooking time: 30 Minutes
Serves: 4 – 1 sandwich per person

Nutrition Facts Per Serving	
Calories	359
Protein	17.1 g
Cholesterol	0 mg
Fat	18.1 g
Carbohydrates	36.6 g
Fiber	5.4 g
Sodium	1532 mg

Ingredients

- 1 large onion, chopped
- 1 medium tomato, chopped
- 4 English muffins, toasted
- 4 cloves garlic, chopped
- 8 ounces button mushrooms, sliced
- 1 14-ounce package firm tofu, drained and cut crosswise into 8 slices
- 2 cups baby spinach leaves
- 1/4 cup apple cider vinegar
- 1/4 cup olive oil

- 3 tablespoons soy sauce
- 1 1/2 teaspoons black pepper, divided
- 1 teaspoon salt
- 1/2 teaspoon dried thyme
- Vegan butter (OPTIONAL)

Directions

1. Set the oven to 450°F and allow it to preheat.
2. Take a shallow baking dish and in it mix together the soy sauce, vinegar, olive oil, and 1/2 a teaspoon of the black pepper with a whisk. Put the tofu slices into the dish in a single layer, making sure they are covered on all sides by the mixture and allow it to marinate for 20 minutes, while turning the tofu occasionally.
3. The baking dish now goes into the oven for 20 minutes, then flip the tofu and let it bake for another 10-20 minutes, until the tofu is crispy and the liquid has mostly been absorbed.
4. As this is going on, coat a large nonstick skillet with oil or cooking spray and in it sauté the onion and garlic over a medium to high heat until the onion begins to soften. This is the time to add in the mushrooms. Now continue cooking until they've browned and then add in the tomato, salt, spinach, thyme and remaining black pepper.
5. Keep stirring until the spinach has wilted and there is no liquid left in the pan. If the vegetables are browning too quickly, be sure to turn down the heat some. Season to taste.
6. Take your muffins, put the (optional) vegan butter on the bottom half, add a dollop of the cooked vegetables as well as 2 slices of the tofu and spread more vegetables on top. All you need to do now is add the other half of the muffin and you're ready to rock!

18. Totally Tofu French Toast

These babies are so tasteful that to say anything about them in something other than French would be disgraceful. They are crème de la crème of the vegan way. They are magnifique, délicieuse and a number of other words I can't quite pronounce (Fortunately, my cooking is better than my French).

Preparation time: less than 5 minutes
Cooking time: 6 Minutes
Serves: 4

Nutrition Facts Per Serving	
Calories	154
Protein	6.4 g
Cholesterol	0 mg
Fat	6.2 g
Carbohydrates	18.9 g
Fiber	1.4 g
Sodium	143 mg

Ingredients

- 8 ounces silken tofu
- 1 ripe banana
- Vegan butter or mild-flavored oil for cooking
- 6-8 slices of bread
- 1/2 cup dairy-free milk
- 1 teaspoon agave or maple syrup
- 1/2 teaspoon cinnamon

Directions

1. Over medium heat, heat a non-stick pan.
2. In the meantime, blend the tofu, cinnamon, dairy-free milk, syrup and banana in a processor until they are smooth. Add more milk or water if it's too thick (do it by the tablespoon to avoid thinning it too much).
3. The mixture goes into a shallow dish that is large enough for you to dip the bread. Cover both sides of the bread with the mixture.
4. Put oil or vegan butter into the skillet, but be careful, it is going to be hot. Then add the soaked bread. It will need about 2-3 minutes per side. You know you're good when the edges begin to turn golden brown
5. It works very well with fresh fruit, powdered sugar, or maple syrup.

19. Brilliant Barbeque Seitan Sandwich

Pulled pork, vegan style, is the way to go when you want to satisfy your urges and your ethics as well. We'd like to say it tastes the same as an actual pulled pork sandwich, but the truth might actually be that it's better. Don't believe me? Go on, try it. But afterwards I expect an apology.

Preparation time: 10 minutes
Cooking time: 6 Minutes
Serves: 6 – one slider per person

Nutrition Facts Per Serving	
Calories	241
Protein	17.5 g
Cholesterol	0 mg
Fat	4.6 g
Carbohydrates	31.7 g
Fiber	1.8 g
Sodium	884 mg

Ingredients

- 4 hamburger buns
- 1 package seitan strips or chunks cut into strips
- 1 small onion, chopped
- 1 cup vegan barbecue sauce
- 1/4 cup water
- 1 tablespoon vegetable oil
- Hot sauce (OPTIONAL)
- Suggested toppings: lettuce, tomato, green pepper, coleslaw, red onions

Directions

1. Put a medium sized nonstick skillet on a medium heat and throw in some oil. When that's hot, add the onion and let it sauté for 5-8 minutes, or until the onion have become soft. Add the seitan, and let it cook until it is lightly browned. Be sure to stir often.
2. Put the barbecue sauce and water in with the Seitan and, while stirring every 5 minutes or so, let it cook until the sauce has been thickened and been absorbed by the seitan. If you're using hot sauce, now is the time to add that in.
3. To prevent the bread from getting soggy when you put in the mixture, toast it, then add the seitan mixture, garnish and serve.

20. Bad Ass Black Bean Soup

This wonderful soup is so full of taste and goodness that you could probably survive off it alone if you had to and you'd probably never ever get bored to boot. As an added bonus, this soup stays good for a few days, so it's easy to prepare beforehand, so that you can have it when the mood strikes. This is a great addition to the busy person's recipe book.

Preparation time: 10 minutes
Cooking time: 20 minutes
Serves: 6-8

Nutrition Facts Per Serving	
Calories	635
Protein	38.1 g
Cholesterol	0 mg
Fat	7.1 g
Carbohydrates	108.1 g
Fiber	26.7 g
Sodium	231 mg

Ingredients

- 1 onion, chopped
- 3 cloves garlic, minced
- 3-4 bay leaves
- 1 green bell pepper, chopped
- 1 can diced tomatoes
- 6 cups black beans, cooked
- 2 cups vegetable broth
- 1/4 cup fresh parsley

- 2 tablespoons olive oil
- 2 tablespoons vinegar, apple cider
- 1 teaspoon ground cumin
- 1 teaspoon ground coriander
- 1 teaspoon smoked paprika
- Salt and pepper to taste

Directions

1. Take a large stockpot, place it over a medium high heat, add olive oil, and sauté the garlic, onion, and bell pepper until the onion begins to soften after about 5 minutes.
2. Now add the vinegar, tomato, coriander, cumin, paprika, salt, pepper and bay leaves and give it another 5 minutes.
3. It is time to put in the beans as well as the broth. Reduce the heat so that the pan is only simmering. Give 15 minutes, with the lid on.
4. Take out the bay leaves, spoon into the bowls and garnish with the parsley.

21. Excellent Egg-free salad Sandwiches

That still taste like it has got egg in it! Yes, that's right. We've tried this one out on our non-vegan friends and they couldn't even tell the difference. Of course, that was a bit of a problem as then they ate it all and we were left with nothing, but then you can't win them all. So it's good that at least this one's a winner.

Preparation time: 10 minutes
Cooking time: 0 Minutes
Serves: 4

Nutrition Facts Per Serving	
Calories	144
Protein	7.7 g
Cholesterol	0 mg
Fat	2.5 g
Carbohydrates	5.5 g
Fiber	1.5 g
Sodium	347 mg

Ingredients

- 1 12-ounce package extra firm tofu
- 1 celery stalk, diced
- 1 small pickle, diced
- 2 green onions, diced
- 1/2 cup vegan mayonnaise
- 2 teaspoons mustard
- 1 teaspoon lemon juice or apple cider vinegar
- 1 teaspoon garlic powder

- 1/4 teaspoon ground cumin
- Salt and pepper to taste
- Indian Black Salt (kala namak) (OPTIONAL)
- Bread, tomato, lettuce, or other desired sandwich fixings

Directions

1. First wrap the tofu in a paper towel then around that wrap a clean dish towel. Place it between two between two heavy pots (one on the top, one on the bottom – not one on the left one on the right) for about 10 minutes. Unwrap the wet dish towel and replace it with a dry one. Put the tofu back between the two pans and give it 5 more minutes.
2. Cut the tofu into irregular pieces.
3. In a bowl, combine the tofu with the mustard, garlic, vegan mayonnaise, cumin and either the lemon juice or the vinegar. Then add in the celery, pickle and onions and season with a bit of salt, pepper and – if you like – black salt. If you are using the black salt, then don't put in too much of the white salt.
4. Toast the bread, then assemble your sandwich and serve.

22. Jack's Terrific Chili

Vegan chili. Not only does it exist, it rocks. Healthy, well rounded and full of fantastic flavors, one you've gone with Jack, you'll never want to go back. We've fed this to people without telling them it was vegan and they loved it (and some refused to believe us when we let the cat out of the bag).

Preparation time: 10 minutes
Cooking time: 1 hour 10 minutes
Serves: 8

Nutrition Facts Per Serving	
Calories	140
Protein	5.9 g
Cholesterol	0 mg
Fat	3.4 g
Carbohydrates	26.6 g
Fiber	8.6 g
Sodium	415 mg

Ingredients

- 2 carrots, chopped
- 1 bell pepper, chopped
- 1 cup frozen corn
- 1 zucchini, chopped
- 1 large onion, coarsely chopped
- 2 15-ounce cans of beans drained and rinsed (kidney, black, pinto, etc.), add a third can of beans if not using vegan crumbles or TVP

- 1 28-ounce can diced tomatoes
- 1 small can tomato paste
- 1/2 cup vegetable broth
- 3 tablespoons chili powder (or more to taste)
- 1 tablespoon vegetable oil
- 2 teaspoons ground cumin
- 2 teaspoons garlic powder
- 2 teaspoons Italian seasoning
- 1 teaspoon salt
- Black pepper to taste
- 1 cup dry TVP or 1 package vegan crumbles (OPTIONAL)
- 1 jalapeño pepper, minced (OPTIONAL)

Directions

1. If you're using the TVP then you should start by heating a couple of teaspoons of vegetable oil in a large nonstick skillet. When the oil is hot, add the TVP and let it toast over medium to high heat, while stirring constantly. It will need about 3 minutes.
2. In a separate pan, bring 1 cup of water or vegetable broth to a boil and then pour it over the TVP. That done the mixture can be put aside.
3. Take a large stockpot, put it over a medium heat and heat a 1 tablespoon of vegetable oil. Then it's time to add the onion and let it sauté for 2 minutes.
4. That done, put in the Jalapeño (if you're using it), the tomato paste, tomatoes, ground cumin, chili powder, garlic powder, Italian seasoning, salt, and pepper. It will need to cook for about 5 minutes.
5. Put in the soaked TVP (if that's what you're using) otherwise, put in the vegan crumblings. In both cases, also put in the carrots, and bell pepper. Put the lid on the pot, turn down the heat and let it simmer for 30 minutes.
6. Now add the corn, zucchini and the beans and let it simmer another 30 minutes, but this time without the lid.
7. Season to taste and serve it with rice or pasta. Vegan Sour cream tastes great overtop.

23. La La La Layered Lasagna

Luscious flavors that linger lovingly as lips are licked in luxurious liking. This one's a feast for all the senses and the tummy to boot. How can you say no to so many layers lovingly arranged, I ask you? You can't. This one has to be tried to be believed.

Preparation time: 30 minutes
Cooking time: 40 Minutes
Serves: 6-8

Nutrition Facts Per Serving	
Calories	372
Protein	26 g
Cholesterol	0 mg
Fat	11.1 g
Carbohydrates	45 g
Fiber	5.9 g
Sodium	793 mg

Ingredients

- 1 14-ounce package extra firm tofu
- 1 package vegan crumbles or 2 cups TVP
- 1 12-ounce package lasagna noodles
- 8 ounces raw spinach
- 6 cups red marinara sauce
- 2 cups vegetable broth, if using TVP
- 1/2 cup vegan mozzarella shreds
- 1 tablespoon lemon juice or white vinegar
- 1 tablespoon olive oil

- 1 teaspoon salt
- 1 teaspoon garlic powder
- 1 teaspoon Italian seasoning
- 1/4 teaspoon ground nutmeg

Directions

1. Set your oven to 375°F and allow it to preheat.
2. Drain the tofu, put it in a mixing bowl and mash it. Then add the salt, Italian seasoning, lemon juice, garlic powder and nutmeg. Let this marinate, as you get on with the next step.
3. If you're using the TVP put it in a bowl and let it soak in the 2 cups of boiled vegetable broth. If you're using the vegan crumbles, take a small frying pan, put it over a medium high heat, add oil and break up the crumble in the pan. Then let it cook for 5 minutes, as you stir occasionally. You're looking for it to turn golden and crispy. Once it does so, you can take it off the heat.
4. Take a 9 x 13-inch pan and spread a thin layer of marinara sauce on the bottom.
5. Take your pasta noodle layers and apply a layer of tofu-ricotta evenly over each of them. Then layer them on the bottom of the pan. Next it's time to create a layer of the spinach leaves, followed by either the TVP or the vegan crumble, create another layer with 1 cup of the marinara sauce.
6. Then do it again in the same order, with the rest of the ingredients, finishing it off with half a cup of vegan cheese.
7. Put some foil over top, put it in the oven and give it 35-45 minutes, until the sauce is bubbling. Take the foil off and give it another 5 minutes in the oven. It will need about 15 minutes to cool, then it is ready to be served.

24. Magical meatless Meatloaf

A triumph of the vegan kitchen, this meatless meatloaf is a feast of flavor that will have eyebrows raised in surprise at the first bite and plates raised in quest for more after the last one. It really is amazing what we can do with the vegan kitchen these days.

Preparation time: 10 minutes
Cooking time: 1 hour
Serves: 4-6

Nutrition Facts Per Serving	
Calories	231
Protein	15.9 g
Cholesterol	0 mg
Fat	8.4 g
Carbohydrates	25.1 g
Fiber	4.5 g
Sodium	1476 mg

Ingredients

- 1 small onion, minced
- 3 cloves garlic, minced
- 1 pound vegan crumbles
- 1/2 cup soft bread crumbs
- 1/2 cup ketchup or tomato paste (divided)
- 1/4 cup dairy-free milk
- 2 tablespoon mustard (divided)
- 1 tablespoon soy sauce
- 1 tablespoon mustard

- 1 tablespoon apple cider vinegar
- 1 tablespoon molasses
- 1 teaspoon horseradish
- 1 teaspoon salt

Directions

1. Set the oven to 350°F and let it preheat.
2. Take all the ingredient listed above EXCEPT for 1/4 cup of ketchup or tomato paste, 1 tablespoon of mustard, the apple cider vinegar and the molasses. Everything else you should combine them in a large bowl. Take a bread loaf pan and line it with parchment paper. The ingredients go into the form. Make sure you press it down firmly.
3. Take the remaining ingredients, namely the 1/4 cup of ketchup or tomato paste, 1 tablespoon of mustard, the apple cider vinegar and the molasses and whisk them together in a separate bowl. Use this to glaze the loaf.
4. Put foil overtop and let it bake for 50 minutes, take off the foil and give it another 10 minutes.

25. Lovely Lemon Garlic "Chicken"

Here the lemon and the garlic serve the chicken flavor fantastically well, creating a wonderful embrace of different tastes that augment each other and prove that sometimes the whole can be better than the parts. Add to that that it's rich in fiber, while being low in calories and it's hard to go wrong.

Preparation time: 20 minutes
Cooking time: 40 Minutes
Serves: 4

Nutrition Facts Per Serving	
Calories	109
Protein	16.6 g
Cholesterol	0 mg
Fat	12.1 g
Carbohydrates	62.4 g
Fiber	10.1 g
Sodium	810 mg

Ingredients

- 8 small red potatoes, quartered
- 6-8 cloves garlic, minced
- 3 sprigs fresh rosemary, de-stemmed
- 2 lemons, 1 cut into thin slices or wedges and 1 juiced
- 1 package of vegan chicken cutlets
- 3/4 pound green beans, trimmed
- 1/4 cup olive oil
- 1 teaspoon salt

- 1/2 teaspoon black pepper

Directions

1. Preheat your oven to 400°F.
2. Take a large baking sheet, put the potatoes on top and toss them, together with a tablespoon of olive oil. Sprinkle some salt and pepper overtop and roast in the oven for 15 minutes.
3. Take a large baking or cast-iron skillet and coat it with 1 tablespoon of the olive oil.
4. Create a single layer with the lemon slice and 1/3 of the rosemary on the bottom.
5. Combine what remains of the olive oil and the rosemary with the garlic, pepper, salt and lemon juice, then add the green beans and mix it all together well.
6. With thongs, take out the green beans and put them on top of the lemon slices as a second layer at the bottom of the baking pan or cast-iron skillet. Next, create a third layer, this one made with the potatoes.
7. Add the vegan chicken to the olive oil mixture bowl and make sure it is thoroughly coated. Then put the chicken mixture on top of the other three layers. Let all of it roast for 20 to 30 minutes, until the green beans are tender, but still bright, while the chicken edges have turned golden brown.
8. Divide the chicken, potatoes and green beans up equally over the plates, top it off with the lemon and serve it hot.

26. Precious Potato Salad

This egg free salad is a great combination of creamy and crunchy, this zesty potato salad balanced perfectly on that edge between sweet and sharp. It's a wonderful way to liven up your starches and don't be surprised if this becomes an indispensable summer fun recipe.

Preparation time: 15 minutes
Cooking time: 10 minutes
Serves: 6

Nutrition Facts Per Serving	
Calories	139
Protein	3 g
Cholesterol	0 mg
Fat	3.4 g
Carbohydrates	25.4 g
Fiber	2.7 g
Sodium	730 mg

Ingredients

- 2 pounds red potatoes, cut into large cubes
- 1/3 cup vegan mayonnaise
- 1/4 cup parsley or chives, finely chopped
- 2 tablespoons Dijon or brown mustard
- 1 tablespoon lemon juice
- 1 1/2 teaspoons salt
- 1 teaspoon black pepper
- 1 cup celery, diced (OPTIONAL)
- 1/4 cup red onion, chopped (OPTIONAL)

Directions

1. Put water in a large pot and let it come to a boil, then add the chopped potatoes and let it cook for 10 minutes, until potatoes are soft enough to be pierced with a fork, but no more than that. Drain off the water and give the potatoes a rinse in cold water, set them aside and let them cool completely.
2. In a small bowl, mix together the mustard, salt, lemon juice, pepper and mayonnaise.
3. When the potatoes have cooled completely, put them into a large bowl. Add in the celery, onion chives and parsley then toss it all through each other. Add in the mayonnaise mixture and mix it up again.
4. Leave it to cool down for 2 hours, put in some more seasoning if you so desire and it is ready to be served.

27. Magnificent Mac & Cheese

Mac and cheese doesn't just have to be something that you used to eat back in college when you had the culinary skill of a wombat. With this recipe you can bring it right back out of retirement and make it a mainstay of your family's week. Who said mac and cheese is dead? Release the cheese!

Preparation time: 5 minutes
Cooking time: 10 Minutes
Serves: 2-4

Nutrition Facts Per Serving	
Calories	545
Protein	41.2 g
Cholesterol	0 mg
Fat	11.9 g
Carbohydrates	77.6 g
Fiber	14.6 g
Sodium	945 mg

Ingredients

- 1/2 pound pasta
- 2 cups dairy-free milk
- 1 cup nutritional yeast
- 1/2 cup vegan cheese shreds
- 1 tablespoon mustard
- 1 tablespoon lemon juice or apple cider vinegar
- 1 tablespoon soy sauce

- 1 tablespoon peanut butter or tahini
- 1 teaspoon garlic powder
- 1/2 teaspoon paprika
- 1-2 teaspoons salt

Directions

1. In one pan, make *al dente* pasta.
2. In the meantime, in a stockpot mix together your lemon juice, peanut butter (or tahini) soy sauce and mustard over a low heat. Then, while whisking, add in the garlic powder nutritional yeast and paprika as well. Continue to whisk as you add in the dairy-free milk until you're at the thickness you want, then add some salt for taste.
3. Add the vegan cheese now is the time. Wait for it to melt completely, turn off the heat, add the pasta and mix it all together. It is ready to be served.

28. Holiday Stuffing

Obviously, you need stuffing. So many festivals depend on it! That's why we've included this beauty here, for you to stick to your guns, while not being forced to sacrifice on flavor. Now if we could only have some vegan turkey, aye?

Preparation time: 10 minutes
Cooking time: 50 Minutes
Serves: 6-8

Nutrition Facts Per Serving	
Calories	317
Protein	6.9 g
Cholesterol	0 mg
Fat	11.2 g
Carbohydrates	50.2 g
Fiber	6 g
Sodium	505 mg

Ingredients

- 1/2 small onion, diced
- 2 celery stalks, chopped
- 2 Fuji, gala, or pink lady apples, cored and chopped
- 4 cups bread cubes, toasted
- 1 cup vegetable broth
- 1/3 cup raisins
- 1/4 cup dried cranberries
- 2 tablespoons vegetable oil (divided)
- 1 teaspoon basil

- 1 teaspoon garlic powder
- 1 teaspoon oregano
- Salt and pepper, to taste

Directions

1. Put your oven on 350°F and allow it to preheat.
2. Take a large nonstick skillet, put in a 1 tablespoon of the oil and let it heat up over a medium to high heat. Throw in the onion and the celery and sauté until it's tender, which should take about 5-7 minutes.
3. The rest of the oil goes into a medium casserole. Make sure the entire surface is coated. Then add the vegetables.
4. Add in the ingredients you haven't used yet and make sure everything is mixed together well, so that the bread cubes, for example, are soaked in the vegetable broth. Put it in the oven for 45 minutes, take it out and it is ready to be served.

29. Chunky Chewy Chocolate Chip Cookies

One of life's greatest joys has to be chocolate, so it's a good thing there's a vegan way to make it. Here we've created a wonderful recipe for chocolate chip cookies, so that you don't have to miss out on those either. These cookies get the two-thumbs up from everybody we've given them to and we've given them to a lot of people.

Preparation time: 10 minutes
Cooking time: 10 Minutes
Serves: 10 – 3 cookies per person

Nutrition Facts Per Serving	
Calories	516
Protein	5.9 g
Cholesterol	0 mg
Fat	28.9 g
Carbohydrates	59.1 g
Fiber	1.9 g
Sodium	405 mg

Ingredients

- 12 ounces dairy-free chocolate chips
- 1 cup vegan butter, softened
- 2 1/4 cups flour
- 1/2 cup white sugar
- 1/2 cup brown sugar
- 1/4 cup dairy-free milk
- 1 teaspoon vanilla
- 1 teaspoon baking soda

- 1/2 teaspoon salt

Directions

1. Put your oven up to 350°F and allow it to preheat.
2. Put the butter, white sugar, and brown sugar in a large bowl and mix until it's all light and fluffy. Then, while you continue to stir, slowly add in the dairy-free milk along with the vanilla. The mixture should turn creamy.
3. Take a small bowl and in it mix together the baking soda, salt and flour. Add this to the first bowl and mix these two things together well as well. The next step is to fold in the chocolate chips.
4. Put the batter onto a nonstick baking sheet in small dollups and let it bake for 8-10 minutes. They are ready to be served.

30. Classic Cupcake with Buttercream Frosting

These awesome cupcakes with fantastic frosting will let you surprise all the other mothers at the next bake sale. For not only are they lower in fat, they're far higher in taste to boot. Great for picnics, desserts or just to share out with tea, these babies are sure to impress.

Preparation time: 10 minutes
Cooking time: 25 minutes
Serves: 12

Nutrition Facts Per Serving	
Calories	434
Protein	3.3 g
Cholesterol	0 mg
Fat	20.7 g
Carbohydrates	60.2 g
Fiber	0.6 g
Sodium	323 mg

Ingredients

- Buttercream Frosting
- 3-4 cups powdered sugar
- 2 cups all-purpose flour
- 1 1/4 cup dairy-free milk
- 1 cup vegan butter
- 3/4 cup sugar
- 1/4 cup vegetable oil
- 3-4 tablespoons dairy-free milk
- 1 tablespoon apple cider vinegar

- 2 teaspoons vanilla extract
- 1 1/2 teaspoons baking powder
- 1 teaspoon vanilla extract
- 1/2 teaspoon baking soda
- 1/2 teaspoon salt
- 1/4 teaspoon salt

Directions

1. First start by preheating the oven to 350°F and add baking liner to the cupcake tins.
2. Slowly mix the vinegar, vanilla and oil into the vanilla and the dairy free milk in a small bowl. It should curdle.
3. Separately, take a large bowl and a fine mesh sieve and sift through the flour, baking powder, salt, sugar and baking soda.
4. Pour the liquid from the first bowl into the second bowl and stir carefully, so that you don't overmix. Once they've been combined, you can carefully add them to the cupcake cups till they're about 2/3 full.
5. Put them in the oven and allow them to bake for 20-25 minutes or until when you put a toothpick in and pull it out again, it comes out clean. Take it from the oven and give it a few minutes to cool. Put the cupcakes on a tray and allow them to cool on a cookie rack.
6. For the frosting, whip the vegan butter, until it has become smooth and soft. Now add in the powdered sugar, while mixing. Do so one cup at a time so that it doesn't clump. The more sugar you add, the thicker the frosting becomes.
7. Add in the salt, vanilla and a small amount of the dairy-free to create the desired consistency. All you need to do now is spread it out over the cooling cupcakes and serve.

31. Freaky Fudge Brownies

These fudge brownies should come with a warning. "These things are highly addictive. Don't serve just before dinner." Sweet, soft and oh so delicious, I've seen plates of these things vanishing quicker than daydreams before a ruler wielding teacher.

Preparation time: 10 minutes
Cooking time: 25-30 Minutes
Serves: 20 – 1 brownie each

Nutrition Facts Per Serving	
Calories	287
Protein	3.1 g
Cholesterol	0 mg
Fat	15.6 g
Carbohydrates	36.2 g
Fiber	1.5 g
Sodium	66 mg

Ingredients

- 2 cups flour
- 2 cups sugar
- 1 cup vegetable oil (1/2 cup can be substituted with apple sauce for a more cake-like brownie)
- 1 cup water
- 1 cup dairy-free chocolate chips
- 1/2 cup cocoa powder
- 1 teaspoon baking powder
- 1/2 teaspoon salt

- 1 teaspoon vanilla
- 1/2 cup chopped walnuts (OPTIONAL)

Directions

1. While you let your oven preheat to 350°F, grease a 9 x 13-inch baking pan.
2. Take all the dry ingredients and combine in a mixing bowl. In a separate bowl, whisk together the oil (or apple sauce) with the water and mix them together with the dry ingredient.
3. Then put in half of the chocolate chips along with the chopped walnuts. The resulting mixture goes into the prepared pan, then sprinkle the remaining chocolate chips overtop.
4. Put them in the oven and give 20-25 minutes. Let them cool and they're ready to be enjoyed.

32. Raging Raw Green Spaghetti

This is the pasta that my carnivore brother always wants to eat when he comes over to visit. In fact, ever since I started making this pasta, he's started coming over a lot more. Do you think that's because he loves me more or because he loves my cooking more? Well they say the way to a man's heart is through his stomach, so I'm not complaining!

Preparation time: 10 minutes
Cooking time: 0 minutes
Serves: 2-3

Nutrition Facts Per Serving	
Calories	437
Protein	10.6 g
Cholesterol	0 mg
Fat	40.7 g
Carbohydrates	14 g
Fiber	5.8 g
Sodium	37 mg

Ingredients

- Squeeze of lemon juice
- 1 clove Garlic
- 2 large Zucchini
- 2 cups fresh Basil leaves
- 1/2 cup Extra Virgin Olive Oil
- 1/2 cup Savory Yeast Flakes
- 3 tablespoon Pine nuts
- 3 handfuls of Snow Peas or Sugar Snap Peas, thinly sliced

Directions

1. In a blender, blend together the oil, garlic, lemon juice, pine nuts, yeast and basil leaves until the resulting mixture is smooth.
2. Turn the zucchini into noodles with a mandolin or Julienne vegetable peeler. The process is one of slicing the zucchini lengthwise to create long strips. Keep turning the zucchini as you work until only the core and the seeds remain. These can be discarded.
3. Mix the "noodles" with the pesto and the snow peas. Season with a bit of pepper and salt and it is ready to be served.

33. Celestial Celeriac Salad

This great little salad only takes 10 minutes to prepare and yet is so chock full of nutrition that you have to wonder how there can be room for the flavor. And yet it's there, in spades, with all the different ingredients combining just perfectly. In fact, just writing about it is making me hungry. Go on without me, I'll be right back.

Preparation time: 10 minutes
Cooking time: 0 Minutes (20 minutes in the refrigerator)
Serves: 4

Nutrition Facts Per Serving	
Calories	108
Protein	1.1 g
Cholesterol	0 mg
Fat	8.2 g
Carbohydrates	7.7 g
Fiber	1.1 g
Sodium	254 mg

Ingredients

- 1 medium celeriac, peeled and coarsely grated
- Juice of 1 lemon
- 2 tablespoon egg-free Mayonnaise
- 1 tablespoon flaxseed oil
- 1 teaspoon dill (fresh or dried)
- 1 teaspoon parsley, roughly chopped
- Sea salt and freshly ground black pepper

Directions

1. Take a medium-sized bowl and in it mix together the lemon juice, mayonnaise, flaxseed oil, parsley and dill. Take the celeriac and fold it through the mixture until it is all well mixed together.
2. Season with pepper and salt, cover and put it in the refrigerator. It will need about 20 minutes, then it is ready to be served.

34. Terrific Cheezy Sauce

Cheezy sauce for vegans; it sounds like an oxymoron and maybe there's an element of slightly-of-hand, but that doesn't change that this beauty is very tasty indeed. It goes very well with paste, tofu and a whole host of other prepared meals. And as it's quite light on the bad stuff, you can really drench your food in it without having to worry about the consequences. Now there's something to be said for that!

Preparation time: 5 minutes
Cooking time: 20 minutes
Serves: 1 cup (nutrition calculations based on 1/2 cup per person)

Nutrition Facts Per Serving	
Calories	285
Protein	13.2 g
Cholesterol	0 mg
Fat	15.2 g
Carbohydrates	26.9 g
Fiber	6.4 g
Sodium	419 mg

Ingredients

- 300ml soymilk
- 1 brown onion, diced
- 1 garlic clove, minced
- Sea salt and freshly ground black pepper
- 3 tablespoon Lotus savory yeast flakes
- 3 tablespoon water
- 2 tablespoon dairy free margarine

- 1 tablespoon rice flour
- 1/2 teaspoon chilli flakes

Directions

1. Take a small bowl, add to it the rice flour and water and mix them together until they form a smooth paste. Put the bowl aside.
2. Take a small saucespan and over a medium heat, melt the dairy-free margarine. You want it to be bubbling ever so slightly.
3. Put in the garlic, onions and chilli and cook until the onion has become soft but has not yet browned.
4. Turn the heat down to low, add the yeast flakes and flour paste until it's all well mixed together.
5. Add in the soymilk a dash at a time, as you stir constantly to make certain it's well mixed and there are no lumps.
6. Now turn up the heat slightly while you continue to stir the sauce. It will take about 5 minutes for the sauce to start to thicken. Add more soymilk if you feel the sauce is becoming too thick.
7. Put in a bit of pepper and salt and it is ready to be served.

Special Tip

- Spinach or kale can be added to increase the dish's nutritional value.

35. Special Spaghetti and Phenomenal Falafel

A good bit of Israeli and Mediterranean fusion, this beautiful recipe takes the best of both worlds and then makes them even better. This works very well as it is and can be enhanced with a few simple little twists and turns, so be sure to experiment and turn it into your own.

Preparation time: 15 minutes
Cooking time: 5 Minutes
Serves: 2-3

Nutrition Facts Per Serving	
Calories	542
Protein	24.8 g
Cholesterol	0 mg
Fat	13 g
Carbohydrates	72.5 g
Fiber	11.1 g
Sodium	353 mg

Ingredients

- Spaghetti
- 2 cloves garlic, crushed
- 2 large handfuls of mushrooms (any kind; I used shiitake and button)
- 1 packet of falafel mix
- 1 large jar of crushed tomatoes/passata
- 1 glass red wine (or water)
- 1/2 red chilli, chopped (or 1/2 teaspoon chilli flakes)
- 1/2 onion, peeled and chopped

- 1/4 cup of walnuts
- 1/4 cup yeast flakes
- 2 tablespoon char-gilled capsicum slices (from a jar, drained)
- 2 teaspoon black olives, drained and chopped
- 2 teaspoon caramelized onions (from a jar)
- Fresh basil leaves

Directions

1. In a large saucepan, bring water to a boil.
2. At the same time, put some coconut oil in a large fry pan and shallow fry the falafel balls for a few minutes, then put them into a small bowl.
3. Throw the onion, garlic and mushrooms into the same frying pan and wait for the juices from the mushrooms to simmer off.
4. Put in the crushed tomatoes, your previously prepared falafel balls and the other ingredients. Then let it stir and simmer while you prepare the spaghetti. (To prepare the spaghetti follow the packet instructions).
5. Put the spaghetti into low bowls then on top pour the falafel balls and sauce. Garnish with fresh basil leaves and serve.
- You can make a fantastic walnut 'parmesan cheese' which you can use as garnish, by combining 1/4 cup savory yeast, 1/4 cup walnuts and a dash of salt in a blender, then mixing them until they form a powder.

36. Perfect Potato and Pesto Soup

This dish makes me so very happy. Initially that was less true of my friends, as I'd made it when they weren't there and couldn't shut up about it for the next few days. They got very annoyed. That all melted away, however, when they finally got to try it themselves. Then they couldn't shut up about it! So good and so yummy, it should be a crime not to try it. Really. I'm trying to get legislation passed.

Preparation time: 15 minutes
Cooking time: 10 minutes
Serves: 3-4

Nutrition Facts Per Serving	
Calories	864
Protein	28.8 g
Cholesterol	0 mg
Fat	54.2 g
Carbohydrates	76.6 g
Fiber	17 g
Sodium	1073 mg

Ingredients

- 3 large potatoes, peeled and chopped
- 2-3 garlic cloves, minced
- Squeeze of lemon juice
- 1/2 small onion, peeled and chopped
- 4 cups vegetable broth/stock
- 2 cups fresh Basil leaves
- 1/2 cup Extra Virgin Olive Oil

- 1/2 cup yeast flakes
- 1/2 cup Pine nuts
- 1 teaspoon vegan margarine

Directions

1. Heat the margarine in a large saucepan and sauté the onion and garlic for 2 or 3 minutes. Add the potatoes to the pan and let it cook for a little longer, then put the vegetable broth into the pan, turn down the heat and allow the dish to simmer until the potatoes have become soft.
2. Combine basil, extra virgin olive oil, pine nuts, nutritional yeast and lemon juice in a blender and blend until it has become smooth.
3. Put aside this mixture and next blend the potatoes and vegetables until they' are smooth and return them to the pan (you might have to do this in several batches).
4. Add the pesto mixture to the soup, add in salt and pepper and it is ready to be served.

Special Tip

- You might want to actually wait one or two days before you eat the soup, as it will taste even better as the pesto flavors spread through the soup.

37. Crazy Cashew Chili con Queso

When you think about it doesn't cashews and chill just make sense? It just goes together like sugar and spice (and everything nice). It's not just true in your imagination either, these two flavors create a feast of flavor on a dinner plate, further augmented by the vegan cheese to turn any occasion where you serve this dish into a Happening. Yes, that's right, with a big 'H'.

Preparation time: 5 minutes
Cooking time: 0 Minutes
Serves: 8

Nutrition Facts Per Serving	
Calories	105
Protein	5.3 g
Cholesterol	0 mg
Fat	6.5 g
Carbohydrates	8.6 g
Fiber	2.6 g
Sodium	75 mg

Ingredients

- 1 garlic clove, crushed
- 3/4 cup raw cashews
- 1/3 cup Savory Yeast Flakes
- 1/3 cup water
- 1/4 cup salsa (we use 'Medium' heat)
- 2 teaspoon chilli powder (optional)
- 1 teaspoon ground cumin

- dash of salt

Directions

1. This one's tough. Put all the ingredients in a blender. Turn it on. Wait until the mixture has turned smooth and creamy. Then turn the blender off.
2. Go take a nice long bath, you deserve it.

38. Fantastic Coconut Fusion Laksa

Laksa is a south East Asian curry dish that is very quickly doing the rounds. And could it not? It's so flavorsome and so delicious that to try it is to remember it and to want it again. In fact, I'm almost jealous of those people that have never tried it before, because they still get to experience this foodgasm for the first time.

Preparation time: less than 10 minutes
Cooking time: 12 Minutes
Serves: 4

Nutrition Facts Per Serving	
Calories	499
Protein	5.8 g
Cholesterol	0 mg
Fat	25.5 g
Carbohydrates	66.4 g
Fiber	3.3 g
Sodium	287 mg

Ingredients

- 1 packet Coconut Fusion
- 1 13 1/2 fl. oz. can coconut milk
- 1 8 1/2 oz. package rice vermicelli
- Fresh cilantro leaves and fresh chili to garnish
- 1 1/4 cup water
- 1 cup bean sprouts
- 1/3 cup or half can of fresh baby corn

- 1/3 cup fresh oyster mushrooms
- 4 tablespoons laksa paste (available at Thai grocery)
- 1 teaspoon fresh grated ginger
- 1/4 teaspoon salt
- 1 bunch bok choy

Directions

1. Cook the lentil mix according to the instructions provided on the packet.
2. In the meantime, slice the bok choy diagonally, the baby corn in half lengthwise and quarter the oyster mushrooms. Let the noodles soak in a bowl of boiling water for a few minutes until they have become tender, then drain away the water. Make sure you get rid of as much as possible.
3. When the lentil mix is ready, put the laksa paste in a frying pan and fry it up in a little oil for 3 minutes. Add in the ginger and let it cook for an additional minute. Put the laksa mix, along with the coconut milk and water, with the lentils and let it come to a boil. Add the vegetables and let the whole thing simmer for 2 minutes.
4. Divide the result over soup bowls and it is ready to be served.

39. Terrific Turmeric Baked Pumpkin

This might well be the prettiest dishes in the book. Served in an actual pumpkin, decorated with flowers and leaves, it is a visual feast that isn't let down by the taste. Add to that that it's so healthy bullets will bounce off you after you've had it and you can't go wrong. I'd say try it next Halloween, but why wait that long?

Preparation time: 10 minutes
Cooking time: 40 minutes
Serves: 4

Nutrition Facts Per Serving	
Calories	78
Protein	2.5 g
Cholesterol	0 mg
Fat	1.3 g
Carbohydrates	16.8 g
Fiber	5.9 g
Sodium	16 mg

Ingredients

- 1 packet Lentil Turmeric Magic
- 1/2 a medium-large pumpkin
- Sweet paprika and/or sumac
- 100 gm salad leaves
- Several nasturtium and begonia flowers or other edible blooms from your garden

Directions

1. Set the oven to 375°F and allow it to preheat.
2. With a spook, scoop the pips out of the pumpkin, thereby creating a hollow in its center
3. Brush the pumpkin with oil and sprinkle the paprika (and sumac if you want) over the top, then put it on an oiled baking tray, and put that in the oven for 30 – 45. You want the flesh to turn soft. This might take longer for some pumpkins than others, depending on the size. Allow it to cool slightly.
4. While the pumpkin is baking, take your lentil mix and prepare it according to the package instructions. Also, wash the salad and flowers.
5. When the pumpkin is cool enough to handle, but still warm take it off the oven tray and put it on a platter. Next, put the hot lentil mixture into the hollow you created when you scooped out the pips. Over top, sprinkle a little freshly ground black pepper.
6. Spread the leaves and flowers out at the base of the pumpkin, to enhance the presentation and serve.

40. Very Vegan Hollandaise Sauce

When I became vegan Hollandaise sauce and all that came with it (basically all of the French kitchen) was a hard thing to give up. Thank the stars that I found this recipe, because suddenly I didn't have to surrender anything. In fact, it let me discover this wonderful concoction all over again, which in some ways made it even better.

Preparation time: 10 minutes
Cooking time: 0 minutes
Serves: 1 cup (nutritional information based on 2 tablespoons)

Nutrition Facts Per Serving	
Calories	150
Protein	5 g
Cholesterol	0 mg
Fat	11 g
Carbohydrates	9 g
Fiber	1 g
Sodium	35 mg

Ingredients

- Zest and juice of 1 lemon
- Pinch cayenne pepper
- 3/4 cup cashew butter
- 2 teaspoons Dijon mustard
- 1 teaspoon garlic powder
- 1/2 teaspoon ground turmeric

Directions

1. Take a blender, put into it 1/2 a cup of warm water, the mustard, cashew butter, lemon zest, garlic powder, lemon juice, turmeric, and cayenne, then let it blend until it's all turned smooth. You might have to add more water to thin the resulting mixture.
2. Put it in an airtight container and refrigerate it for 3 days. It is ready to be used.

41. Precious "Pork" and Coriander Dumplings

The Chinese haven't yet really figured out this entire vegetarian thing, let alone the vegan thing, so it can be a bit hard to enjoy their kitchen. Fortunately, we're not going to let that hold us back. If they won't adapt their kitchen, then we will and we'll make it better than it ever was in the process. Who's with me?

Preparation time: 15 minutes
Cooking time: 10 Minutes
Serves: 6 – 5 dumplings per person

Nutrition Facts Per Serving	
Calories	74
Protein	4.5 g
Cholesterol	0 mg
Fat	2.8 g
Carbohydrates	7.5 g
Fiber	1 g
Sodium	238 mg

Ingredients

- 3 mini pork-style sausages
- 1 finely chopped spring onion (shallots)
- Handful coriander leaves
- 1 small chilli
- Ginger
- pinch sugar
- pinch salt
- 1 tablespoon lemongrass

- 1 tablespoon garlic
- 2 teaspoons lime juice to taste
- 1 packet egg-free wonton wrappers

Directions

1. Using a mortar and pestle mix together the lemongrass, chilli, and garlic to create a spice paste. Add the chilli a little at a time, until the paste has the right spiciness for you.
2. Add in the finely chopped coriander leaves, along with the sugar, salt and lime juice.
3. Blend the sausage in a food processor until you've got a coarse mince.
4. In a nonstick frying pan heat a dash of oil, then stir-fry the mince with a bit of spring onion. Then add in the earlier-made paste until the taste is strong and delicious. Put it aside and let it cool.
5. Create a work station to make your dumplings. You'll need a bowl of water for you to dip your fingers in, your dumpling wrappers all stacked up, a board for you to fold you dumplings on, and your fillings with a teaspoon so that you can easily scoop the content into the dumpling.
6. Put a teaspoon of the filling in the center of a dumpling wrapper. Wet your fingers and moisten the edge of the wrapper then fold it up into a triangle. Crimp the edges, then press the filling outwards to remove air pockets. Put the dumpling aside and proceed to the next dumpling.
7. When all your dumplings are ready, let a pan of salted water come to a boil and add the dumplings to the water. Don't throw in too many! A few will do. Wait about 2 minutes, until the pastry becomes translucent. Take the dumpling out with a slotted spoon and set it aside. Dumplings work well with an assortment of sauces, including just plain soy sauce.

42. Terrific Tofu Feta Cheese

Here's a fantastically simple recipe that will have you gobbling down vegan feta cheese in no time. And you get to practice your forearms as well! A workout and cheese for over the pasta, whatever more do you want? Fifteen minute preparation time? You've got it!

Preparation time: 15 minutes
Cooking time: 10 minutes
Serves: 4

Nutrition Facts Per Serving	
Calories	63
Protein	5.9 g
Cholesterol	0 mg
Fat	3 g
Carbohydrates	63 g
Fiber	1.5 g
Sodium	10 mg

Ingredients

- 1 1/2 liquid quarts fresh soy milk
- 1 1/2 teaspoon food-grade epsom salts in 1/2 cup just boiled water
- Olives, chopped
- Italian herbs, to taste
- 1 tablespoon tahini
- 1/2 teaspoon miso paste
- 1/2 cup savory yeast flakes
- Ground black pepper, to taste

Directions

1. Take freshly made soy milk (if you can, commercial soy milk will also work, so long as it has no additives besides soybeans and water) and heat it until it comes to a boil. Turn off the heat and stir the soymilk into boiling water which already contains the epsom salts already dissolved inside. Cover the pan with a lid and let it sit for 10 minutes.
2. When you lift off the lid, you should see clouds of curd floating in the water. These are what you're after. Use a strainer to place this curd either into a strainer or into a couple of clean tea towels.
3. Once the curd is drained but still moist, put it into a bowl and add the other ingredients. Then put it in a muslin and press and shape it into a block.
4. These blocks go into the refrigerator for several hours. You'll know it's ready when it has a crumbly texture.

Special Tip

- You can also try changing the flavor by including such ingredients as grilled capsicum/peppers, sundried tomatoes, fresh peppercorns, or dried fruit.

43. Fast Vegan Chicken Burger Quick Meal

Sometimes you just feel like a burger, well here you go! This burger will satisfy that urge without leaving behind our ethics. A great number that is so ridiculously simple to make you could almost do it while you're sleep walking (there are flames involved, so it might be best if you don't actually try).

Preparation time: 10 minutes
Cooking time: 5 Minutes
Serves: 1

Nutrition Facts Per Serving	
Calories	228
Protein	9.7 g
Cholesterol	0 mg
Fat	15.3 g
Carbohydrates	14 g
Fiber	3.2 g
Sodium	126 mg

Ingredients

- 1 Vegan Chicken Burger patty
- Slice of Notzarella vegan cheese
- 1 wholemeal bread roll
- Salad greens
- A handful of salad greens
- Cherry tomatoes, quartered
- A handful of mixed salad sprouts
- 1/4 of an avocado, diced

- 2 tablespoons of cooking oil (olive oil, sunflower oil, etc.)
- Hamburger Sauce (your choice)

Directions

1. Put oil in a frypan and after the oil is warm, place the Vegan Chicken Burger in side.
2. As you cook both sides of the patty lightly, slice the bread roll in half. Then place the cooked burger patty on one half.
3. Put the Notzarella cheese on top. Add the greens and your favorite sauce. Close the bun. Mix the greens, the cherry and the salad sprouts. Throw the avocado pieces over top and it is ready to be served.

44. Chirpy "Cheesy" Lasagna

A terrific dish that is full of calcium, magnesium, vitamins and taste to boot. This one will impress the savages as well as the rest of us, so serve it when you've got family over that haven't yet been converted. If any dish can tip the balance, then it is this one.

Preparation time: 30 minutes
Cooking time: 45 minutes
Serves: 4

Nutrition Facts Per Serving	
Calories	125
Protein	5.2 g
Cholesterol	0 mg
Fat	1.9 g
Carbohydrates	65.3 g
Fiber	9.2 g
Sodium	90 mg

Ingredients

- Mountain bread (8 sheets)
- 250ml tomato puree
- 3 medium carrots
- 1 large capsicum
- 1 bunch of bok choy (or other spinach if you prefer)
- 1 tomato
- 1/2 large eggplant
- 1/2 small onion
- 1/2 tub Vegan Ricotta Cheese

- 1/2 jar Pesto
- 1/4 butternut pumpkin
- 1/4 block Notzeralla
- I sprig oregano leaves
- 1 teaspoon ground nutmeg
- 1/2 teaspoon ground pepper

Directions

1. First slice the pumpkin and the carrots and then put them under the grill for 10-15 min so that they've become slightly soft. Slice up the capsicum and the eggplant as well, to the same thickness as the pumpkin and the carrots. The tomatoes need to be sliced up as well. Dice the bok choy, both the stalks and the leaves, as well as the onions.
2. Take a backing tray and create a layer with 2 of the mountain bread slices. Put capsicum and the eggplant mixed together with half of the tomato puree on this layer of bread. Spread it out so that it two forms an even layer.
3. Create another layer of the mountain bread, again using two slices. Spread the pesto on top of this layer of bread, making sure that all of the bread has been covered. Now make a layer with the pumpkin and the carrot, again make sure it's even.
4. Time for another 2 sheets of mountain bread and on top of that spread the tofutti cheese thickly and evenly.
5. Sprinkle some nutmeg and pepper over this layer, then add the bok choy and the onion to create yet another layer on top of that.
6. Create your final level of mountain bread, pressing down on the whole thing slightly to compact it. Spread the remaining tomato puree over top. Then create a layer with the sliced tomato, the oregano leaves and the finely grated Notzerella.
7. Take some alluminium foil, spray it with cooking oil to avoid having the cheese stick to it, put it on the baking tray and then bake the whole thing in an oven of 220 degrees for 35 to 40 minutes.

Special Tip

- Please note that the lasagna will compact and shrink as it cooks, so in order to have it retain its form as much as possible, make sure you compact it before you put it into the oven.

45. Vegan Fish with Awesome Orange Sauce

In this dish, the orange and the Vegan fish work together so beautifully it might just be able to bring a tear to your eye. That's alright, you can always pretend it's for the company rather than the food – great taste and brownie points. What more could you want?

Preparation time: 20 minutes
Cooking time: 20 Minutes
Serves: 2

Nutrition Facts Per Serving	
Calories	62
Protein	0.9 g
Cholesterol	0 mg
Fat	6.9 g
Carbohydrates	11.7 g
Fiber	2.5 g
Sodium	78 mg

Ingredients

- 6 pieces Lamyong Vegan Chunky Fish, thawed
- 1 navel orange
- Salt
- Pepper
- 1 tablespoon grated orange rind
- 1 tablespoon red wine vinegar
- 1 tablespoon vegetable oil

Directions

1. Zest the orange, peel it and squeeze it for juice. In a bowl, mix the orange rind and juice with the red wine vinegar, the salt and the pepper. Set this aside.
2. Take a nonstick frying pan and heat the oil over a medium to high flame. Use the orange zest mixture to coat the sides of the vegan fish, then put the fish in the pan. Make sure you turn over the fish and baste it as you go.
3. Take the fish out, pour the rest of the sauce into the pan and turn up the heat. While stirring constantly, let the sauce cook for a bit, so that it thickens.
4. Pour the sauce over the vegan fish and serve immediately.

46. Righteous Red Lentil Soup with Pumpkin

This dish is just a circus of flavor, with the lentil, pumpkin, masala and curry powder combining into a flavor feast. Add to that that it is filled to the brim with such things as fiber, iron, manganese and magnesium and it's hard to imagine how you could go wrong here.

Preparation time: 10 minutes
Cooking time: 30 minutes
Serves: 4

Nutrition Facts Per Serving	
Calories	348
Protein	17.4 g
Cholesterol	0 mg
Fat	5.5 g
Carbohydrates	62.5 g
Fiber	26.5 g
Sodium	639 mg

Ingredients

- 50 ounces pumpkin
- 1 cup of red lentils (uncooked)
- 1 onion
- 4 cloves garlic, crushed
- 2 Chicken Style stock cubes
- Salt to taste
- 1 tablespoon olive oil
- 1 teaspoon cumin

- 1 teaspoon garam masala
- 1 teaspoon dried thyme leaves
- 1 teaspoon tumeric
- 2 teaspoons curry powder
- 1 teaspoon cayenne pepper

Directions

1. Chop up the onions, as you allow the oil to heat in a large saucepan. Cook the onions and the garlic in said saucepan until the onion is soft (about 2 to 3 minutes). Next, put in all the spices and mix them till they're wonderfully fragrant.
2. Take the skin off the pumpkin, scoop out the seeds and chop the flesh up roughly (as in so that you have rough chunks, not as if you're Freddy Kreuger). Put the pumpkin in with the red lentils and onion mixture. Add water till the pumpkin is just submerged. Add in the chicken style stock cubes and mix it well. Add a bit of salt if you so desire and bring it up to a boil. Lower the heat, so that the pan is simmering and wait for the pumpkin to go soft and the red lentils to be cooked.
3. Put the content in a blender and blend until it has turned soft. It is ready to be served.

47. Princely Piñata bowls

These layered bowls of wholesome goodness will knock your socks off, even as they'll fill you up to the brim. Not for the faint hearted, these are some big bowls. You could even decide to share them out between three if your appetites can't handle this amount of food. Or you can turn it into a bit of an eating contest and show who is the boss, vegan style.

Preparation time: 10 minutes
Cooking time: 10 Minutes
Serves: 2

Nutrition Facts Per Serving	
Calories	600
Protein	15.7 g
Cholesterol	0 mg
Fat	17.4 g
Carbohydrates	97.9 g
Fiber	12.9 g
Sodium	767 mg

Ingredients

- 1/2 green or red capsicum
- 1 small onion
- 2 tomatoes, chopped
- 1/2 head iceberg lettuce, chopped
- 1 carrot, grated
- 1 avocado, sliced or smooshed
- Sprinkle of salt or Vegie Parmesan
- 1 box of chicken-style strips, thawed

- 1 cup uncooked brown rice
- 2 tablespoon water
- 1 tablespoon soy sauce
- 1 tablespoon barbeque sauce

Directions

1. Chop up the Fry's chicken-style strips into slightly smaller chunks, then put them in a bowl, together with the barbecue sauce, soy sauce and water and mix it together well. Let the strips marinate for a while.
2. Follow the package instructions to cook the brown rice.
3. In the meantime, take a frying pan, put in a little oil and cook both the capsicum and the onion (which should take about 3 minutes). When they are done set them aside.
4. Slice and dice your tomatoes and lettuce and grate your carrot. Set this to the side as well.
5. The fry Fry's chicken-style strips plus the remaining marinade now go into the frying pan, where you cook them over a medium heat for about 5 minutes. (Microwaving them for 2-3 minutes also works).
6. When the rice is done drain out any remaining water and mix in the capsicum and the onion.
7. Take your bowls, add a layer of the rice mixture, flatten it out, then add a layer of the Fry's chicken-style strips. Create a third layer with the carrot, tomato and lettuce. Top each bowl off with sliced or smooshed avocado. Add a sprinkle of salt, as well as a bit of vegan Parmesan. It is ready to be served.

48. TVP Meatloaf

You won't taste the difference! It's that good! This dish makes use of Textured Vegetable Protein to create a fantastic substitute for those of us who need a bit of umani but don't want others to have to suffer for it. Leftovers work very well as sandwiches.

Preparation time: 10 minutes
Cooking time: 50 Minutes
Serves: 8

Nutrition Facts Per Serving	
Calories	149
Protein	12.1 g
Cholesterol	0 mg
Fat	4.1 g
Carbohydrates	17.9 g
Fiber	2.3 g
Sodium	599 mg

Ingredients

- 2 stock cubes dissolved in 2 1/2 cups of boiling water
- 1 finely chopped onion
- 3 cups of TVP mince
- 3/4 cup whole meal flour
- 1/2 cup of tomato sauce
- 1/2 cup of finely chopped parsley
- 2 teaspoon basil
- 2 teaspoon cooking oil
- 1 teaspoon salt

- 1 teaspoon marjoram
- 1 teaspoon oregano
- 1 teaspoon garlic powder
- 1/2 teaspoon pepper

Directions

1. In a bowl, mix together the TVP, water, stock, tomato sauce and basil, then let it stand for 10 minutes
2. Take a nonstick skillet, put it over a medium to high heat and add a bit of oil. Then sauté the onion until it turns translucent, after about 2 to 3 minutes. Add to TVP mix and stir it all together.
3. Take it off the fire and add in all the other ingredients you haven't used yet.
4. Take a loaf pan, oil it lightly and pack in the mixture. Make sure it's tight.
5. Put the loaf pan in a preheated oven at 350°F and give it 45 minutes. Take the pan out and let it cool for 10 minutes before you take out the meatloaf.
6. Best served with roasted vegetables and gravy.

49. Cool Cachapas

This dish has been adapted from the original Venezuelan recipe. Now if there's one area in the world where you might be hard pressed to survive as a vegan, then it is in South America. After all, they put us Americans to shame in their meat-eating quantities, but with dishes like this you can level the playing field and possibly convert some of the locals to our side!

Preparation time: 7 minutes
Cooking time: 20 Minutes
Serves: 3

Nutrition Facts Per Serving	
Calories	437
Protein	21.1 g
Cholesterol	0 mg
Fat	21.1 g
Carbohydrates	48.9 g
Fiber	8.4 g
Sodium	671 mg

Ingredients

- Jalapenos to taste
- Cherry Tomatoes
- Salt and Pepper to season
- 3 cups fresh corn
- 1 cup Mozzarella-style cheese (or any that will melt)
- 3/4 cup almond or soy milk
- 2/3 tablespoon plain flour

- 2 tablespoon ground flaxseed
- 2 tablespoon sugar
- 1/2 teaspoon baking powder
- 1/2 teaspoon salt

Directions

1. In a food processor, mix together the corn, flour, milk, ground flaxseed, baking powder, sugar and salt and pulse until you've got something that looks like creamed corn. You can add in extra milk if you think it is too thick. Let the batter stand 10 minutes, while you stir occasionally.
2. Put a large non-stick frypan on a medium heat and coat it with cooking spray.
3. Scoop out about a 1/4 cup of batter, pour it into the pan and spread it out, by 'rolling' the pan. Give it 3 to 4 minutes to cook, then flip it. Spread out some of the shredded jalapenos, cheese, and sliced cherry tomatoes on the cooked side and let it cook for 2 to 3 minutes.
4. Add seasoning and fold over the pancake, like it's an omelet. Give it another minute and it is ready to be served. Repeat the process with the rest of the batter.

50. Tofu and Lovely Vegetable Laksa

Another laksa to titillate the taste buds, when I have to make Laksa I never know which way to go – should I go with this one or the other? I think the flavor of this one might be a little bit more authentic, which might matter to those of us that have actually been out to the exotic east, but as to which one is better, I honestly can't tell you.

Preparation time: 15 minutes
Cooking time: 15 hour
Serves: 4

Nutrition Facts Per Serving	
Calories	601
Protein	20.8 g
Cholesterol	0 mg
Fat	21.1 g
Carbohydrates	81.7 g
Fiber	5.8 g
Sodium	2954 mg

Ingredients

- 2 cups of water
- 1 Massel vegetable or chicken flavored stock cube
- Bean sprouts
- Mixed vegetables (eg. baby corn, snow peas, mushrooms and broccoli)
- Fresh coriander and chilli
- Half a packet of fried tofu puffs (from Asian grocery stores)
- 13 1/2 ounces can of coconut milk
- 3 1/2 ounces packet of dried bean vermicelli

- 1 1/2 tablespoon of vegan Laksa paste (for a mild Laksa; use more for a hotter paste)

Directions

1. Put the bean vermicelli in cold water and let it soak for 15 minutes.
2. In the meantime, put water in large saucepan, then add the stock and stir well to get it to dissolve. Bring the water to a boil.
3. Put in both the Laksa paste and coconut milk. Again, let it come to a boil while you're stirring. Add in the vegetables and the tofu and let the whole mixture cook for 5 minutes.
4. Take the vermicelli, drain off the water and share it out between two large soup bowls. Put in the laksa and cover with a hand-full of bean sprouts.

51. Coquettish Quinoa Croquettes

These beautiful, yummy and crispy croquettes work wonderfully as appetizers. They're low in calories and fat and therefore won't prevent you from choosing a more luxurious main, while still being full of unique flavors. Of course, you don't have to have them as appetizers. They work equally well as snacks or as sides.

Preparation time: 15 minutes
Cooking time: 1 hour
Serves: 14

Nutrition Facts Per Serving	
Calories	94
Protein	4 g
Cholesterol	0 mg
Fat	1 g
Carbohydrates	18 g
Fiber	3 g
Sodium	139 mg

Ingredients

- 6 garlic cloves, minced
- 2 cups corn, frozen (10 ounces of frozen corn kernels)
- 2 cups no-salt-added vegetable broth (or water)
- 1 cup black beans, cooked, rinsed, drained
- 1/4 cup green onions, chopped (the whole onions)
- 1 teaspoon sea salt (divided)
- 1/2 teaspoon sea salt
- 1/8 teaspoon cayenne

- 1/4 cup ground pumpkin seeds (OPTIONAL)
- 1 tablespoon ground flax seed (OPTIONAL)

Directions

1. Start off by washing the quinoa well. Take a medium sauce pan, put it on a medium to high flame and add the quinoa, garlic, 1/2 a teaspoon of sea salt and cayenne. Put the lid on and wait for it to boil, then turn down the heat and let it simmer for 15 to 20 minutes.
2. Stir in the other 1/2 teaspoon of salt, corn, flaxseed, green onions, black beans and (the optional) pumpkin seeds.
3. Take a baking tray and cover it with parchment paper (oil will work as well). Be aware that these croquettes can be very stick, so parchment paper is the safer option.
4. Once the quinoa mixture has cooled enough for you to handle it take about 2 tablespoons in your hands per time, shape it into log-like shapes and place it on the baking sheet. Continue until done. If this is difficult because the mixture is too dry, it is fine to add some water. If, on the other hand, it is too moist, use brown rice flour to thicken it.
5. For a brown crispy crust, spray some cooking oil over them. Turn the oven up to 400°F and put them inside (preheating isn't necessary). Let it bake for 35 minute, or until they are light golden brown and have crispy edges.

52. Perfectly Roasted Portobello Mushroom Pate

A gorgeous pate that can keep for weeks (if it ever lasts that long), this recipe works well for mains, snacks and appetizers. The best way forward is simply to make a lot once a month and then bring it out on special occasions, when you need something more. Note that the sizes mentioned here are for appetizers, if you use it as part of a main, the nutritional information will be a little different.

Preparation time: 20 minutes
Cooking time: 1 hour (+2 or 3 to bake in the flavors)
Serves: 16

Nutrition Facts Per Serving	
Calories	170
Protein	8 g
Cholesterol	0 mg
Fat	8 g
Carbohydrates	18 g
Fiber	5 g
Sodium	232 mg

Ingredients

- 7 garlic cloves
- 1 1/2 pounds Portobello mushrooms with stem
- 1 medium onion
- 3 1/2 cups water
- 1 3/4 cups mung beans, washed and drained
- 3/4 cup walnuts
- 2 tablespoons dark miso

- 2 teaspoons olive oil
- 1 teaspoon sea salt
- 1/2 teaspoon olive oil
- 1/4 teaspoon ground black pepper
- 1/4 teaspoon sea salt (or more to taste)
- 1/4 cup flax oil (OPTIONAL) (do not use if this dip is to be baked)

Directions

1. Remove the stems from the Portobello mushrooms, clean them with a brush and gently wash them, but don't use too much water as the caps are like sponges. Wash the stems separately.
2. Cut the Portobello caps into 1/2-inch pieces. Chop up the stems as well. Throw all the pieces into a bowl, along with the olive oil and 1 teaspoon of salt.
3. Cover a baking tray with parchment paper, put the Portobello pieces on top and roast them at 450°F. You do not need to preheat the oven. Give them about 25 minutes. You're looking for them to be completely dried out.
4. Put a pressure cooker without a lid over medium-high heat and add the oil. When it is hot, sauté the onions until they brown just slightly. Put inside the washed mung beans as well as water, seal the cooker let the pressure build.
5. Turn on the timer and adjust the heat so that the pan is only simmering. Let it cook for 20 minutes.
6. Take the pot from heat, release the pressure and open her up.
7. In a food processor, grind the walnuts. Put in the mushrooms, beans and the remaining ingredients. Blend this mixture until it has turned smooth. You can change the consistency with either broth or water if you like. It will thicken when refrigerated.
8. You can serve it immediately, or you can refrigerate it. If you go for the second option, then bake at 250°F for 1 to 2 hours to let the flavors fully integrate.

53. Seriously Stuffed Mushrooms

Question: What's better than mushroom? Answers: mushrooms stuffed and overflowing with goodness! In this dish the tofu and the mushrooms accent each other beautifully, creating these wonderful little bundles that can serve as party snacks, or as appetizers (obviously, they won't serve 30 when you use them like that and so the nutritional information will be slightly different).

Preparation time: 10 minutes
Cooking time: 1 hour
Serves: 30

Nutrition Facts Per Serving	
Calories	29
Protein	2 g
Cholesterol	0 mg
Fat	2 g
Carbohydrates	2 g
Fiber	1 g
Sodium	101 mg

Ingredients

- 12 1/3 ounces silken tofu, blended
- 2 pounds mushrooms, whole (about 60 large button mushrooms)
- 1 large onion, chopped fine
- 1 1/3 cups chopped celery, chopped fine (from about 3-4 stalks)
- 1 tablespoon olive oil
- 1 1/2 teaspoon sea salt (divided)
- 1 1/2 tablespoons olive oil

- 1 teaspoon ground thyme
- 1/2 teaspoon ground sage

Directions

1. Take the mushrooms and wash and stem them. Put the mushroom caps in a small bowl and put them aside. Chop the mushroom stems finely.
2. Place a pot over medium-high heat and add oil. When the oil is hot, sauté the onion for a few minutes, then add in the stems and cook until they've lost all their moisture. Put in the celery as well and give it a few more minutes to cook. It should take about 20 minutes for them all to be done. Add in the sage and the thyme and mix it all up. Remove it from the heat and fold in the smoothly blended tofu as well as 1/2 a teaspoon of sea salt.
3. Take the mushroom caps, add oil and 1/2 teaspoon of sea salt, then with a teaspoon press the filling (i.e. the original mixture) into each mushroom cap. As the mushrooms will shrink in the oven, don't overfill them.
4. Take a baking tray, cover it with parchment and place the filled mushrooms on to it. Turn your oven to 400°F and bake the mushrooms for 30-40 minutes, or until browned. They are ready to be served.

54. Perky Sweet Potato "Fries"

Sweet potatoes might actually work better as fries than normal potatoes. I kid you not. The sweetness of the potato creates an entirely different experience that adds an extra dimension both in taste and nutritional goodness that the ordinary fries simply lack. The result? You don't need ketchup and the salt that comes with it!

Preparation time: 10 minutes
Cooking time: 50 hour
Serves: 24

Nutrition Facts Per Serving	
Calories	62
Protein	1 g
Cholesterol	0 mg
Fat	1 g
Carbohydrates	13 g
Fiber	1 g
Sodium	46 mg

Ingredients

- 3 1/2 pounds sweet potatoes (cut like thick fries)
- 2 tablespoons maple syrup
- 1 1/2 tablespoons extra virgin olive oil
- 1 teaspoon ground cinnamon
- 1/2 teaspoon sea salt

Directions

1. In a bowl, mix together the potatoes, cinnamon, salt and oil.
2. Cover a baking sheet with parchment paper and spread out the sweet potatoes (the fries are very sticky, so oil doesn't work quite as well).
3. Turn your oven up to 450°F and let them bake for 50 minutes. You want the potatoes to have softened and have become light brown. After 20 minutes make sure you toss the potatoes every 10 minutes or so, to make sure they don't burn.
4. Take them out of the oven, drizzle maple syrup over top and serve.

55. Beloved Black Bean and Vegetable Stew

When I first tried this dish at a friend's house I was a little upset. I thought he'd fed me meat, you see. It's the Seitan that did it. It gives the dish very meaty texture that together with the thick flavors of the stew for a moment had me believe my friend was no friend. Of course, when he'd sworn up and down it was vegan, it didn't take me long at all to make sure it was all gone.

Preparation time: 10 minutes
Cooking time: 30 Minutes
Serves: 8

Nutrition Facts Per Serving	
Calories	173
Protein	13 g
Cholesterol	0 mg
Fat	2 g
Carbohydrates	29 g
Fiber	9 g
Sodium	344 mg

Ingredients

- 14 ounces tomatoes, low sodium
- 1 large red bell pepper, diced
- 4 garlic cloves, minced
- 2 large onions, diced
- 5 carrots, diced
- 2 cups black beans, cooked, drained
- 1 1/2 cups no-salt-added vegetable broth (or water)

- 1 cup corn, frozen
- 1 cup chopped celery (from about 3 stalks)
- 3/4 cup green onions, chopped fine (about 6 stalks)
- 3 tablespoons cilantro, chopped fine
- 2 tablespoons dried basil
- 1 tablespoon tamari soy sauce
- 1 tablespoon cumin powder
- 2 teaspoons dried oregano
- 1 1/2 teaspoons olive oil
- 3/4 teaspoon ground fennel seeds
- 1/4 teaspoon cayenne (or more to taste)
- 1/4 teaspoon sea salt
- 8 ounces prepared seitan, cubed (OPTIONAL)

Directions

1. Put a pot with oil over a medium-high heat. When the oil is hot, giving each of the vegetables a few minutes to sear closed, add the onions, then the carrots, a few minutes later add the celery. A few minutes after that it's time to put in the bell pepper. It's important that all the vegetables have been sealed as otherwise they won't hold their flavor.
2. Put in the garlic, which will need 2 minutes. Add the cumin powder, oregano, cayenne, fennel seeds, and basil and cook for 2 minutes more. Next it's the turn of the corn, tomatoes, seitan, beans, broth and salt. Let the resulting mixture simmer for a little over 10 minutes.
3. Just before you serve it, stir in tamari. For garnish use cilantro and green onions.

56. Generous Collard-Gazbanzo Soup

This quick, creamy, hearty and low-fat soup is done in a jiffy and works beautifully as an appetizer. This is doubly true if you've got a salad for a main, as it just fills your heartiness need. If you want to avoid the gluten in this one, you can replace the oats with rolled grains.

Preparation time: 15 minutes
Cooking time: 20 minutes
Serves: 6

Nutrition Facts Per Serving	
Calories	93
Protein	2.6 g
Cholesterol	0 mg
Fat	8.1 g
Carbohydrates	4.4 g
Fiber	1.5 g
Sodium	58 mg

Ingredients

- 1 3/4 pounds collard greens, chopped (thick stems removed and no long stringy pieces)
- 2 medium onions, chopped
- 5 garlic cloves, minced
- 4 cups no-salt-added vegetable broth (or water)
- 2 1/2 cups garbanzo beans, cooked, rinsed, drained
- 1 cup rolled oats (quick cooking or regular)
- 1 tablespoon olive oil
- 1/2 teaspoon ground black pepper

- 4 teaspoons ground coriander
- 1 1/4 teaspoons sea salt

Directions

1. Place a pot over a medium-high heat. Add the oil and sauté the onion and garlic for about 10 minutes. Then put in the coriander and pepper and give it another 2 minutes. Add the oats and salt and allow it to cook an additional 2 minutes. Finally, add in the beans and broth and let it simmer for 5 minutes, until the oats are cooked.
2. Put the chopped collars in a steamer and give them 3 minutes to soften, then add them to the soup.
3. Put the soup in a blender and blend until smooth.
4. It is ready to be served.

57. Charming Creamy Cauliflower Soup

This wonderful soft soup is sure to impress! It's creamy, delicious, nutritious and oh so good! While the cauliflower is the obvious ingredient, in this case it's the almonds that give it its depth. A depth that is far greater than you'd expect for something this quick and this simple. This one's a winner in our family and makes a regular appearance.

Preparation time: 10 minutes
Cooking time: 30 Minutes
Serves: 6

Nutrition Facts Per Serving	
Calories	109
Protein	4 g
Cholesterol	0 mg
Fat	7 g
Carbohydrates	10 g
Fiber	4 g
Sodium	334 mg

Ingredients

- 2 medium onions, quartered
- 3 1/2 cups no-salt-added vegetable broth (or water)
- 3 cups cauliflower, roughly chopped (about 1 head - florets + core chopped)
- 3/4 cup green onions, chopped fine
- 1/2 cup almonds, chopped
- 2 tablespoons cilantro, chopped fine
- 1/2 tablespoon rosemary (not ground)
- 1 teaspoon sea salt

- 1/2 teaspoon olive oil

Directions

1. Put a pressure cooker without a lid on medium-high heat, with the oil inside. Sauté the onion for about 8 minutes. Put in the cauliflower and let it cook for 9 minutes until it has started to brown slightly.
2. Put the rosemary in a cheese cloth and tie it closed, so that it can't escape. Then, along with the broth, salt, and almonds, add it to the pressure cooker.
3. Cover the pressure cooker and let the pressure build, adjusting the heat so that the pressure is maintained. Give it about 10 minutes. Take the pot from the heat, let the pressure escape and open her up.
4. Take out the rosemary wrapped in cheese cloth from the soup.
5. Pour everything else into a blender and blend it until it is smooth.
6. Garnish with a bit of cilantro and green onions and it is ready to be served.

58. Hospitable Hot and Sour Soup

Sometimes you just want something different. Enter this hot and sour soup, made after Chinese specifications, but without the Chinese need to put dead animal in everything. The lemony sour and the cayenne pepper combine to give this dish a good kick that will put hair on your chest without putting a dent in your diet.

Preparation time: less than 15 minutes
Cooking time: 40 Minutes
Serves: 8

Nutrition Facts Per Serving	
Calories	174
Protein	9 g
Cholesterol	0 mg
Fat	6 g
Carbohydrates	25 g
Fiber	5 g
Sodium	1078 mg

Ingredients

- 1/2 pound baby bok choy (white part cut into matchsticks and green part shredded very thin. The different parts are used in different parts of recipe)
- 1/4 pound mushrooms, thinly sliced
- 16 ounces firm tofu (pressed to remove as much water as possible)
- 6 kaffir lime leaves (or use 1 teaspoon of minced lime zest)
- 2 stalks fresh lemon grass (cut in half and then into 4 inch pieces)
- 2 medium onions, chopped fine
- 3 medium carrots, cut into matchsticks

- 1 medium red bell pepper, cut into matchsticks
- 4 garlic cloves, minced
- 14 ounces canned tomatoes, pureed
- 2 1/2 cups fresh pineapple, cubed (about half of one whole pineapple)
- 2 cups no-salt-added vegetable broth (or water)
- 3/4 cup green onions, chopped fine
- 1/4 cup fresh basil, chopped fine
- 1/4 cup fresh basil, chopped
- 6 tablespoons white miso
- 4 tablespoons brown rice vinegar
- 3 tablespoons tamari soy sauce
- 2 tablespoons unrefined granulated sugar
- 1 tablespoon ginger juice, fresh (squeezed from fresh, grated ginger root)
- 1 tablespoon dark (toasted) sesame oil
- 1 tablespoon dehydrated lily flowers, chopped (AKA dried tiger lily buds)
- 1 teaspoon ground black pepper
- 1/2 teaspoon sea salt
- 1/8 teaspoon cayenne pepper (or to taste)

Directions

1. Put a large pot with oil over medium-high heat. When the oil is hot, add the mushrooms and let them sauté for a few minutes, then put in the onions and give it another 5 minutes. Put in the carrots and cook for a minutes more. Put in the bell pepper, which will need 2 minutes and finally add in the white part of baby bok choy, along with the garlic and cook all these vegetables for a final 2 minutes.
2. Tie the lemon grass in a cheese cloth, make sure it's well tied so the lemon grass can't escape. Then, along with the broth, cayenne pepper, tomatoes lily flower, lime leave, pineapple, tofu and salt, put them in the pan. Let it all come to a boil, then turn down the heat and let it simmer for 25 minutes. Add water or broth if you want it to be more like a soup, rather than a stew.
3. When done, take out the lemongrass as well as the lime leaves. Finely shred the green parts of the baby choy and stir them into the soup.
4. Take out one cup of soup and put it in a bowl. Add the ginger, miso, pepper, sugar, soy sauce, rice vinegar and finely chopped basil. Stir well until the miso dissolves, then add it back into the soup pan and mix it through the soup.
5. Sprinkle some basil and green onions over top and it is ready to be served.

59. Awesome Asian Sweet Potato Salad

In this dish the sweet of the potato clashes wonderfully with the daikon garnish, thereby giving you a mouth full of texture and flavor. Add to that the ginger and it really is one of those dishes that make the Asian cuisine so special. And it smells great too!

Preparation time: 15 minutes
Cooking time: 50 Minutes
Serves: 8

Nutrition Facts Per Serving	
Calories	209
Protein	3 g
Cholesterol	0 mg
Fat	4 g
Carbohydrates	42 g
Fiber	5 g
Sodium	384 mg

Ingredients

- 1 pound daikon, shredded (one large daikon is about one pound)
- 3 1/2 pounds sweet potatoes (about 4 large sweet potatoes)
- 3 tablespoons maple syrup
- 1 1/2 tablespoons dark (toasted) sesame oil
- 1 tablespoon lime juice (zest and juice from one lime)
- 1 tablespoon ginger juice, fresh (squeezed from fresh, grated ginger root)
- 1 2/4 teaspoon sea salt (divided)
- 1 teaspoon dark (toasted) sesame oil
- 1 teaspoon lime zest, chopped

Directions

1. Take a bowl and in it mix the daikon and 1/2 teaspoon of salt. Press them together and let them sit in a cool room, or in the refrigerator. When you want to serve it, drain the liquid.
2. Wash the sweet potatoes and rub them both with oil and 1/2 a teaspoon of salt. Cover a baking tray with parchment paper, lay the potatoes on top and bake them at 350°F for 40-50 minutes until they've turned soft but not mushy, as they will continue to bake once you've taken them out of the oven. Let them cool and then place them in the refrigerator overnight.
3. Remove the potato peel and slice the potatoes up. Then place the sliced potatoes in a large bowl.
4. Mix together the sesame oil, maple syrup, lime zest and juice, 3/4 teaspoon of sea salt and ginger juice in a small bowl.
5. Pour the marinade over the sweet potatoes and then gently mix it up. Put them in the fridge for another 2 hours.
6. It is ready to be served (don't forget the daikon).

60. Quality Quinoa Salad

This quickly prepared Asian-flavored salad isn't just full of tang and goodness, but is also incredibly versatile. This means that it can be eaten as a main, a snack, or on the go, by simply wrapping it in a Chapatti or tortilla. Oh and it's filling too!

Preparation time: 15 minutes
Cooking time: 15 minutes
Serves: 6

Nutrition Facts Per Serving	
Calories	614
Protein	11 g
Cholesterol	17 mg
Fat	37 g
Carbohydrates	65 g
Fiber	6 g
Sodium	638 mg

Ingredients

- 6 garlic cloves, diced into pea sized pieces
- 4 small Chioggia beets, cut into 1" pieces
- 2 small sweet potatoes, cut into 1/2" pieces
- 1 medium onion, chopped
- 4 1/2 cups water
- 2 cups arugula leaves, chopped
- 1 1/2 cups quinoa, washed
- 1 cup garbanzo beans, cooked, rinsed, drained

- 2 tablespoons olive oil
- 1 teaspoon sea salt
- 1/2 teaspoon sea salt
- 3/4 recipe 15-Yuzu-Umeboshi Plum Dressing (see recipe in book)
- 1/2 cup edamame, frozen, shelled, thawed (OPTIONAL)

Directions

1. Take a pot, add water and 1 teaspoon of salt. When the water is boiling, add in the quinoa and stir it all through each other. Let it boil for 10 to 12 minutes (the longer it boils, the softer the texture).
2. Let the grain cool.
3. In the meantime, in a large bowl mix together the beets, potatoes, garlic and onions with oil. Make sure everything is well coated then add a bit of salt and then mix it again. Take a baking tray, cover it with parchment paper and spread out the vegetables in a single layer. Put them in the oven and let them roast until the vegetables are lightly browned. Stir the vegetables occasionally.
4. Add the vegetables to the quinoa. Stir in the arugula and the (optional) edamame as well.
5. Add the dressing (see Yuzu-Umeboshi Plum dressing in this book) and serve.
6. You can refrigerator it up to a week if you don't add the dressing.

61. Terrific Tempeh "Tuna" Salad

This quick "tuna" salad uses dulse to give you that 'under the sea' flavor that is normally quite hard to come by in the vegan kitchen. The salad goes very well on bread and can be used as a dip as well. It's wonderful when a recipe is this versatile, isn't it? Therefore, I suggest always having a bowl ready in your refrigerator for when the mood strikes.

Preparation time: 10 minutes
Cooking time: 10 minutes (needs several hours in the refrigerator)
Serves: 6

Nutrition Facts Per Serving	
Calories	253
Protein	17 g
Cholesterol	0 mg
Fat	15 g
Carbohydrates	20 g
Fiber	1 g
Sodium	547 mg

Ingredients

- 1 garlic clove, crushed
- 16 ounces tempeh, thawed
- 1 cup Nayonaise vegi dressing
- 1 cup carrots, finely chopped (about 2 medium carrots)
- 3/4 cup celery, finely chopped (about 3 medium stalks of celery)
- 1/3 cup green onion, finely chopped (about 2 stalks of green onions; the white and most of the green)
- 1 tablespoon white miso

- 1 tablespoon prepared mustard
- 1 teaspoon dried dill
- 1/2 teaspoon powdered dulse
- 1/2 teaspoon ground black pepper
- 1/4 teaspoon sea salt

Directions

1. Steam the tempeh for 20 minutes.
2. In the meantime, mix together the miso, mustard, garlic, sea salt, dulse, black pepper, vegi dressing and dried dill in a large bowl.
3. Allow the tempeh to cool, then chop it up finely. Add it to the large bowl and toss.
4. Add in the celery, green onion and carrots. Refrigerate for several hours and then you can serve it.

62. Yuzu-Umeboshi Plum Dressing

This unique dressing goes great with green-leaf salads, giving you a distinctly Asian and exotic flavor to what elsewise might end up being just another boring bowl of green. A great choice for the foodies, this is a sophisticated dressing for a sophisticated pallet.

Preparation time: 10 minutes
Cooking time: 0 minutes
Serves: 12

Nutrition Facts Per Serving	
Calories	190
Protein	trace
Cholesterol	0 mg
Fat	19 g
Carbohydrates	7 g
Fiber	Trace
Sodium	72 mg

Ingredients

- 6 ounces flax or hemp oil
- 2 ounces sesame oil, preferably unrefined
- 1 pinch xanthan gum (to thicken the dressing)
- 1/4 cup brown rice vinegar
- 1/4 cup brown rice syrup
- 1/4 cup yuzu juice (or bottled yuzu seasoning base)
- 1 tablespoon umeboshi plum paste

- 1/8 teaspoon sea salt

Directions

1. Get a glass jar that's air tight and put all the ingredients except the xantham gum into it, then give it a good shake to mix it all together.
2. Put the mixture plus the xantham, which will thicken the dressing, into a food processor and blend to a coarse texture.
3. Rather than blending it all the way, put it back into the jar and shake it up again so that not everything is chopped too finely. This will make the dressing far more enjoyable.

63. Original Orange-Ginger Spritzer

This refreshing spritzer is so easy to make and yet so very, very tasty. The combination of orange, ginger and bubbles turn every sip into a tiny sparkly party in your mouth. Add to that that it's full of the good stuff and you will wonder how before you knew of this recipe you ever made do with all the bland drinks out there.

Preparation time: 5 minutes
Cooking time: 0 Minutes
Serves: 4

Nutrition Facts Per Serving	
Calories	94
Protein	1 g
Cholesterol	0 mg
Fat	Trace
Carbohydrates	24 g
Fiber	Trace
Sodium	16 mg

Ingredients

- 8 cups sparkling water
- 1 cup fresh orange juice (from about 2 oranges)
- 1/4 cup light agave nectar syrup
- 4 teaspoons ginger juice, fresh (squeezed from fresh, grated ginger root)

Directions

1. Mix all the ingredients together, then put it in refrigerator to cool for a short time (not too long as the fizz will go).
2. It is ready to be served.

Special Tip

*   You can also use lime juice, though in that case you might need to sweeten the drink more.

64. Magnificent Peach Mango Ice Tea

Maybe in this case the 'tea' should be in quotation marks, for though this might taste like it, it comes with only a fraction of the caffeine, something that is achieved by using the stem of the plant rather than the leaf. After all, the stem contains just as much flavor but won't keep you up at night. This means that this baby works just beautifully as a bed-side drink, which is just an awesome place for this brilliant little number.

Preparation time: 5 minutes
Cooking time: 5 minutes
Serves: 4

Nutrition Facts Per Serving	
Calories	149
Protein	1 g
Cholesterol	0 mg
Fat	trace g
Carbohydrates	37 g
Fiber	1 g
Sodium	46 mg

Ingredients

- 12 ounces frozen concentrate peach-mango juice
- 3 quarts water
- 1/4 cup kukicha twig tea
- 1/2 cup fresh basil, ripped
- 1 tablespoon masala chai tea leaves

Directions

1. Bring water to a boil in a low pot. Turn down the heat, put in the tea and allow it to simmer for 5 minutes. Take it off the fire and strain out the tea.
2. Tear up the basil leaves and add them to the water. Give it 5 more minutes, then strain out these leaves as well. Add the juice and put it in the refrigerator.
3. Let it cool until you're satisfied and it is ready to be served.

Special Tips

- You can use any kind of juice, really. Experiment!
- Ginger will add a little bit of kick.
- Try other teas for different flavors.

65. Cozy Carambola Chutney

Carambola or starfruit chutney, is a way to turn an ordinary meal into something special. The sweet flavors of the chutney create a great counterbalance to the more savory flavors that normally accompany mains and since it's incredibly low in fat, the extra dimension to your meal comes at no extra cost!

Preparation time: 5 minutes
Cooking time: 10 Minutes
Serves: 16 per person

Nutrition Facts Per Serving	
Calories	62
Protein	1 g
Cholesterol	0 mg
Fat	trace
Carbohydrates	16 g
Fiber	3 g
Sodium	32 mg

Ingredients

- 3 cups carambola, sliced (~2 large fresh carambolas)
- 3/4 cup grapefruit peel, sliced
- 1 cup dried figs, diced
- 1 tablespoon lemon juice
- 1 tablespoon apple cider vinegar
- 3 tablespoons brown rice syrup
- 2 tablespoons unrefined granulated sugar (or any granulated sugar)
- 2 tablespoons candied ginger root, chopped

- 1/4 teaspoon sea salt

Directions

1. Put all the ingredients in a saucepan, and the lid on top. Over a medium heat allow it to come to a simmer.
2. Let the chutney thicken to proper consistency.
3. It is ready.

Special Tip

- You can store the chutney for about 3 weeks.

66. Brilliant Basil-key Lime Dressing

A wonderfully tangy dressing for any salad or tofu dish that is so good, you'll soon have it on standby in your kitchen. After all, lime and basil are a great accompaniment to almost any dish. Heck, we even like it on ice cream!

Preparation time: 10minutes
Cooking time: 0 minutes
Serves: 16

Nutrition Facts Per Serving	
Calories	143
Protein	trace g
Cholesterol	0 mg
Fat	14 g
Carbohydrates	6 g
Fiber	trace g
Sodium	118 mg

Ingredients

- 10 garlic cloves, crushed
- 8 ounces flax or hemp oil
- 1 teaspoon sea salt
- 1 pinch xanthan gum (creates a thicker consistency)
- 1 1/2 cups fresh basil, chopped (about one large bunch)
- 1/4 cup brown rice syrup
- 6 tablespoons key lime juice

Directions

1. Get a glass jar that's air tight and put all the ingredients except the xantham gum into it, then give it a good shake to mix it all together.
2. Put the mixture plus the xantham, which will thicken the dressing, into a food processor and blend.
3. Put the mixture back in the jar and shake again. Doing this will give it more texture as some of the ingredients will not be chopped up so fine.

67. Raspberry-Almond Pastry

It looks pretty and tastes even better. This crispy pastry with warm raspberry almond filling is going to impress both the lookers and the triers! Rich in calcium, it works well for special occasions, for dessert or even just for a snack.

Preparation time: 1 hour (30 minutes active)
Cooking time: 20 Minutes
Serves: 10

Nutrition Facts Per Serving	
Calories	380
Protein	9 g
Cholesterol	0 mg
Fat	14 g
Carbohydrates	60 g
Fiber	7 g
Sodium	103 mg

Ingredients

- 5 ounces frozen raspberries
- 2 1/2 cups spelt flour
- 1/2 cup soy milk (divided)
- 3/4 cup brown rice syrup (divided)
- 3/4 cup almonds, chopped
- 1/2 cup poppy seeds, ground
- 1/4 cup maple syrup
- 1/3 cup warm water
- 3 tablespoons vegetable, coconut or sunflower oil, shortening, non-hydrogenated

- 2 tablespoons brown rice syrup
- 2 tablespoons warm water
- 2 tablespoons almond slivers
- 2 tablespoons lemon juice (from about one lemon)
- 1 tablespoon lemon zest, chopped (from about one lemon)
- 1 1/2 teaspoons active baker's yeast
- 1/2 teaspoon sea salt

Directions

1. Put both the yeast together in a bowl and wait about 10 minutes for the yeast to become active. In a separate bowl, mix together the salt and flour, then cut the shortening (or oil) into flour mixture with a fork and a knife.
2. Mix together a 1/4 cup of rice syrup, a 1/3 cup of soy milk and the maple syrup and then add it and the yeast mixture to the flour.
3. Knead the dough for 15 minutes. You might need to add water or soy milk to thin it if the dough gets too dry or stiff. Give the dough 2 hours to rise.
4. In the meantime, make the filling. In a sauce pan combine together a 1/2 cup of the rice syrup, a 1/4 cup of soy milk, the almonds, poppy seeds, lemons zest and juice. Let it cook for 10 minutes, then take it off the heat, add the frozen raspberries and mix it together well. This should defrost the raspberries.
5. Let the mixture cool.
6. Take a baking sheet and cover it with parchment paper. Take the dough and punch it down, then form it into a flat rectangle of about 11 by 13 inches. Put it onto the tray.
7. With a knife, make regular cuts along the dough at about 45 degrees about an inch apart on both sides so that you get long angular strips. These cuts should not reach the center (the center will form the base of the pastry).
8. Put the filling along the middle and then fold the long strips overtop, alternative left than right, so that you get a hatch pattern.
9. Leave the dough to rise for 30 minutes in a warm, moist environment.
10. Preheat the oven to 350°F.
11. To make the glaze, combine 2 tablespoons of rice syrup and the water, then brush it over the pastry.
12. When the oven is hot, put in the pastry and bake for 20 minutes.
13. It is ready to be served.

68. Pretty Pink Grapefruit Sorbet

Sorbets are the way to go if you want that ice-creamy goodness, without that ice-creamy waistline. This grapefruit sorbet isn't just low in fat, but it's also easily adapted to many other types of fruit, making it versatile as well. We just love the tartness of the grapefruit, however, so that's why we wrote it up with that as our fruit of choice.

Preparation time: less than 10 minutes
Cooking time: 0 Minutes (needs several hours in the freezer and 30 minutes in the ice cream maker)
Serves: 8

Nutrition Facts Per Serving	
Calories	114
Protein	1 g
Cholesterol	0 mg
Fat	Trace
Carbohydrates	29 g
Fiber	Trace
Sodium	17 mg

Ingredients

- 1 pinch sea salt
- 2 1/2 cups fresh squeezed pink grapefruit juice (from about five small grapefruits)
- 1 cup white grape juice
- 1/3 cup granulated sugar (preferably light in color)
- 1/4 cup light agave nectar syrup
- 2 teaspoons grapefruit zest, chopped (from 1/2 of a grapefruit)
- 2 teaspoons grapefruit zest (from 1/2 of a grapefruit)

Directions

1. The sorbet ingredients all need to be as cold as possible.
2. Put all the ingredients in the blender and blend them for about 3 minutes.
3. Put the mixture in the freezer for a few hours to give your ice cream maker an easier time of it.
4. Follow the manufacturer's specifications about how to use the ice cream maker itself. It takes about 30 minutes on average, but it might take longer or shorter.
5. Sprinkle the lemon zest over top. It is ready to be served.

69. Precious Peanut Butter-Chocolate Chunk Cookies

So good and yet modest in their calorie count I think these beautiful balls of scrumptious deliciosity have actually been declared illegal in some dictatorships for fear of showing the people that paradise is possible. Fortunately, we live don't live there and can have as much peanut butter and chocolate goodness as we can stomach. Oh to be free!

Preparation time: 10 minutes
Cooking time: 6 Minutes
Serves: 24

Nutrition Facts Per Serving	
Calories	235
Protein	5 g
Cholesterol	0 mg
Fat	12 g
Carbohydrates	28 g
Fiber	2 g
Sodium	176 mg

Ingredients

- 85 grams chocolate, bittersweet, dairy-free, cut in chunks
- 1 1/2 cups brown rice flour or whole wheat pastry flour
- 1 cup peanut butter
- 1 cup unrefined granulated sugar
- 3/4 cup maple syrup
- 1/2 cup chopped peanuts
- 1/2 cup sorghum (or whole wheat pastry) flour
- 1/2 cup vegetable oil spread, non-hydrogenated

- 1/4 cup soy (or whole wheat pastry) flour
- 1 tablespoon vanilla extract
- 1 teaspoon cinnamon (or nutmeg for something different)
- 3/4 teaspoon baking soda
- 1/2 teaspoon baking powder (double acting)
- 1/4 teaspoon sea salt

Directions

1. Turn the oven to 350°F and let it heat.
2. On a baking tray, spread out parchment paper.
3. In a large bowl, mix together the rice flour, sorghum flour, soy flour, sea salt, baking soda, baking powder and cinnamon.
4. In a food process, combine the maple syrup, peanut butter, sugar and vegetable oil.
5. Add the dry mixture to the processor as well and mix thoroughly.
6. Put the dough in a bowl. Knead it while adding in the peanuts and chocolate chunks.
7. Create little balls of dough and spread them out over the baking sheet. Then put the sheet in the oven and bake for about 15 minutes. If you are afraid of the cookies burning, cover them with an additional baking sheet.
8. Let the cookies cool for a few minutes, then put them on a cooling rack so that the air can circulate underneath. After they've firmed up, you can remove them from the parchment.
9. Serve immediately or freeze them, if you like.

70. Perfect Gluten Free Pie Crust

This useful recipe gives you a delicious pie crust that you can use for both sweet pies as well as savory quiches. You can bake the crust on its own and then fill it up with bake-free goodies, or you can include whatever fantastic filling you've got along with the crust in the oven. Give a person a pie, you feed them for a day, give them a pie crust recipe and you feed them for a lifetime.

Preparation time: 15 minutes
Cooking time: 30 minutes
Serves: 8

Nutrition Facts Per Serving	
Calories	242
Protein	4 g
Cholesterol	0 mg
Fat	15 g
Carbohydrates	24 g
Fiber	2 g
Sodium	62 mg

Ingredients

- 1 cup brown rice flour
- 1/2 cup sesame seeds, ground (or pecans, ground)
- 1/3 cup sorghum flour (or brown rice flour)
- 6 tablespoons vegetable shortening, non-hydrogenated (coconut oil and oleic sunflower oil are also possible choices)
- 4 tablespoons water (possibly more)
- 2 tablespoons tapioca flour

- 1/4 teaspoon sea salt

Directions

1. Take a pie dish and oil it. Take the flour sesame seed, tapioca and salt and mix them in a bowl. Next, cut the shortening (or oil) into this mixture with a fork and a knife. Add water and mix it well. The aim is for the dough to be wet enough that it sticks together when you press it, so that it will form a ball easily. This might mean you need to add more water than is included in the ingredient list. Still, better to be safe than sorry and up with a too watery dough, so start with the advised amount.
2. Put the dough into a pie dish and press it gently out across the bottom, so that it forms an even layer. With a fork, poke holes into the crust, to avoid it puffing.
3. The pastry itself will need to be baked for 25-30 minutes at 350°F. If your filling needs longer, then that's fine. Alternatively, if your filling does not need to be baked, then you can add it in after the pastry has cooled.

71. Majestic Maple Cake

This base recipe can be made as is, or can be a platform from which you can launch your madcap experiments into the depths of the vegan culinary arts. Try it out with different fillings, different frosting and different schemes. Don't forget to cackle 'it's a live' every so once in a while when a recipe works out. You know, for the sake of appearances.

Preparation time: 15 minutes
Cooking time: 35 minutes
Serves: 20

Nutrition Facts Per Serving	
Calories	364
Protein	6 g
Cholesterol	0 mg
Fat	17 g
Carbohydrates	50 g
Fiber	3 g
Sodium	167 mg

Ingredients

- 14 ounces coconut milk (or water)
- Lemon-Ginger Icing (see the recipe later in this book)
- 2 1/2 cups brown rice flour
- 1 1/2 cups maple syrup
- 1 1/2 tablespoons vanilla extract
- 1 cup sorghum flour (or brown rice flour)
- 1 cup walnuts, toasted, glazed
- 1/4 cup high oleic sunflower oil (or coconut oil)

- 1/4 cup water
- 1/4 cup unrefined coconut oil (or other oil)
- 4 tablespoons tapioca flour
- 4 tablespoons applesauce, unsweetened (alternatively throw 1/3 of an apple in a blender)
- 1 tablespoon baking powder (double acting)
- 1 teaspoon citrus zest, in long, thin strips (from half of a citrus fruit)
- 3/4 teaspoon sea salt
- 1/8 teaspoon baking soda

Directions

1. Turn your oven to 350°F and allow it to preheat.
2. Take 2 round spring form pans, and oil and flower them. If you don't have spring form pans, you can also use 9 by 9 inch square pans.
3. Sieve the rice flour, sorghum flour, tapioca flour, sea salt, baking powder and baking soda into a large bowl.
4. Separately, combine the sunflower oil, coconut oil, applesauce, maple syrup, vanilla extract and coconut milk. Then add the dry mixture to the liquid. Mix it well and pour it into the prepared cake pans.
5. Put them in the oven and give them 25-35 minutes. Test them by sticking in a toothpick and seeing if it comes out fairly clean of batter. If so take out the cakes. Make sure you don't overbake them as they become too dry and heavy.
6. Take one of the cakes and put it on a serving plate. Put a good layer of frosting on top, then lay the second layer over that and frost this one as well. (see Lemon-ginger frosting for a good frosting recipe)
7. Sprinkle citrus zest and toasted glazed walnuts or pecans over top.

72. Mind-blowing Macadamia Nut Cream

This smooth and creamy dessert is the answer if you've got a cookbook of standard cakes that don't cater to your vegan needs. By replacing the heavy creams with this one, all those recipes are suddenly available to you again. Have your cakes and eat theirs too.

Preparation time: 10 minutes
Cooking time: 2 minutes
Serves: 18

Nutrition Facts Per Serving	
Calories	49
Protein	Trace
Cholesterol	0 mg
Fat	3 g
Carbohydrates	7 g
Fiber	Trace
Sodium	7 mg

Ingredients

- 1/2 cup macadamia nuts, raw
- 1/2 cup water
- 1/4 cup brown rice syrup
- 3 tablespoons maple syrup
- 1 pinch sea salt

Directions

1. Put all the ingredients in a blender and let it run until the content is completely smooth (this will take about 5 to 10 minutes).
2. Put the content in a heated saucepan and let it simmer for 2 minutes.
3. Refrigerate until it is ready to be served (It will keep for about a week).
4. Serve with any pie or pastry (one serving is about 1 tablespoon)

Special Tip

- Instead of macadamia you can use pine nuts, pecans, walnuts or cashews for a similarly smooth finish. Other nuts don't work quite as well.

73. Keen Kahlua-Chocolate Chunk Ice Cream

Kahlua, chunky chocolate and ice cream in one recipe. How can people ever expect us to eat dinner again? Delicious to the last spoonful and capable of giving you a tiny buzz to boot. This is awesomeness in an ice cream scoop. One drawback is that the alcohol means the ice cream needs to be very cold to freeze completely and will melt quickly, so make sure to keep it in the freezer as much as possible.

Preparation time: 20 minutes
Cooking time: 7 Minutes (needs several hours in the freezer and 30 minutes in the ice cream maker)
Serves: 8

Nutrition Facts Per Serving	
Calories	381
Protein	5 g
Cholesterol	0 mg
Fat	17 g
Carbohydrates	51 g
Fiber	2 g
Sodium	28 mg

Ingredients

- 85 grams chocolate, bittersweet, dairy-free, cut in chunks or 3/4 cup dairy-free chocolate chips
- 1 pinch sea salt
- 1 1/4 cups cashews, raw (optionally soaked for a couple of hours, and then drained and rinsed)
- 1 1/2 cups white grape juice

- 1 cup water
- 1/2 cup Kahlua
- 1/4 cup brown rice syrup
- 1/4 cup maple syrup
- 1/4 cup + 2 tablespoons of unrefined granulated sugar (divided)
- 2 tablespoons chopped nuts, toasted
- 2 teaspoons lecithin
- 1 teaspoon vanilla extract
- 1/4 cup coconut milk (OPTIONAL)
- 1 teaspoon kudzu (OPTIONAL)

Directions

1. In a blender, combine the cashews, grape juice, water, rice syrup, maple syrup, 1/2 cup of sugar, lecithin, sea salt and – if you like, the coconut milk and/ or kudzu. Put the blender to high and wait for the mixture to become smooth. Occasionally during this process turn off the processor and scrape the sides, so that everything gets blended. This should take about 7 minutes – possibly longer if your blender is a bit slower.
2. Put the mixture in a sauce pan, put it on a medium to low heat and let the custard thicken while you continuously stir with a wire whisk. This will take about 8 minutes.
3. Add the vanilla extract and the Kahlua.
4. Put the mixture in the freezer. When it is frozen, add it to your ice cream maker. Then follow the manufacturer's specifications. Generally it will take about 30 minutes.
5. As the ice cream maker does its work, melt the chocolate in a small saucepan, then stir in the 2 tablespoons of sugar. When the ice cream is nearly done, drop in tiny drops of this mixture and mix them in (the chocolate should freeze instantly).
6. Scoop the ice cream out into bowls and serve with toasted nuts.

74. Remarkable Roasted Root Vegetables

Sometimes you've just had enough of steamed vegetables, cooked vegetables or the raw variety as well. Then you need a recipe like this to give them that extra bit of flavor to remind you why you're doing all this again. Heck, maybe you'll find you reminding yourself about once a day, when you realize how easy this recipe is.

Preparation time: 10
Cooking time: 50 minutes
Serves: 8

Nutrition Facts Per Serving	
Calories	199
Protein	4 g
Cholesterol	0 mg
Fat	1 g
Carbohydrates	44 g
Fiber	6 g
Sodium	264 mg

Ingredients

- 3 1/2 pounds sweet potatoes, cut into 2" pieces (about 4 large sweet potatoes)
- 2 large carrots, cut into 1" pieces
- 5 garlic cloves, crushed
- 2 large potatoes, cut into 2" pieces
- 1 large onion, thinly sliced
- 2 tablespoons dried dill weed
- 1 1/2 teaspoons olive oil
- 1 teaspoon sea salt

Directions

1. Take a bowl and add the vegetables, dill, oil and salt.
2. Spread parchment paper over a baking sheet
3. Spread out the vegetables over the sheet in a single layer and put them in an oven at 450°F. Let them bake for 50 minutes or until the vegetables have both softened and browned. Make sure to toss the vegetables repeatedly during the last 30 minutes as otherwise they'll burn.

Special Tips

- If you add celery for the last 30 minutes your vegetables will have a nice bit of crunch.
- Change out the dill with basil, garam, or rosemary – or go really experimental and try masala, for something different.

75. Orange Glazed Broccoli with Carrots and Kale

By glazing the vegetables with this orange glaze, you end up adding an entirely new unexpected side to the taste, without adding any further to your waistline. This recipe is fruit and vegetable in one genius, wholesome combination that will make every dinner a treat.

Preparation time: 10 minutes
Cooking time: 10 Minutes
Serves: 6

Nutrition Facts Per Serving	
Calories	132
Protein	6 g
Cholesterol	0 mg
Fat	2 g
Carbohydrates	26 g
Fiber	5 g
Sodium	378 mg

Ingredients

- 1 large onion, diced
- 3 carrots, sliced
- 1 pound kale, chopped (or collards)
- 4 cups broccoli florets
- 1 cup broccoli stalks, slivered (read directions)
- 1 cup orange juice (fresh squeezed from about 2 oranges)
- 4 tablespoons sorghum flour (or brown rice flour or spelt flour)
- 1 tablespoon ginger juice, fresh (squeezed from fresh, grated ginger root)

- 1 tablespoon sweet sherry (or mirin)
- 1 teaspoon olive oil
- 1 teaspoon sea salt

Directions

1. Take the broccoli, cut the stalks away from the florets, gather those that are the tenderest and sliver them.
2. Place a nonstick skillet on a medium to medium high heat, put in the oil and sauté the onion for several minutes. Add the slivered broccoli stalks and continue cooking until the onions have browned. This should take about 7minutes.
3. As this is going on make the glazing mixing the juices, flour and sherry. Set this aside for a moment.
4. Turn back to the pan and add the carrots, give it a few more minutes, then add the broccoli florets. After another 3 minutes throw in the kale. This won't take long at all to cook. Add the salt and the glazing.
5. Let it cook for a few more minutes to let the glazing thicken, then take it off the fire and it is ready to be served.

76. Hearty Greens and Charming Chickpea Sauté

In this dish the vegetables are sautéed, thereby keeping both the flavor and the nutritional goodness. This is a great way to show doubters that it is possible to cook greens in a way that is utterly appetizing and might well convince them that there's more to our kitchen than they'd ever thought possible.

Preparation time: 10 minutes
Cooking time: 15 minutes
Serves: 8

Nutrition Facts Per Serving	
Calories	153
Protein	8 g
Cholesterol	0 mg
Fat	2 g
Carbohydrates	26 g
Fiber	8 g
Sodium	297 mg

Ingredients

- 2 large onions, chopped
- 3 medium carrots, sliced
- 3 pounds mixed hearty greens, chopped (e.g. collards, kale, and/or chard) (leaves only)
- 1 1/2 cups garbanzo beans, cooked, rinsed, drained
- 3/4 cup red wine
- 2 tablespoons unrefined granulated sugar
- 1 teaspoon olive oil

- 1 teaspoon sea salt (divided)

Directions

1. Take a nonstick skillet, add oil and heat it over a medium-high heat. Sauté the onions for 7 minutes, then add in the carrots and cook for another 4 minutes. Add the hearty green mixture and cook until everything is done.
2. As the vegetables are doing their thing in the skillet, mix together the chickpeas, 1/2 a teaspoon of salt and the sugar in a small pan. Then cook the mixture until there is no liquid left. This will give a sweetened red wine flavor to the chickpeas.
3. When vegetables are done add 1/2 a teaspoon of salt and stir it in, then add the chickpeas mixture and cook for about 1 minute.
4. It is ready to be served.

77. Lovely Lemon-ginger Icing

Lemon, ginger and almost no fat combine in this flavorsome yet easy-to-make icing to brilliant effect. The tartness, sweetness and ginger kick will turn even the plainest of cakes into slices of heaven. Note, the icing works even better if it's left overnight in the fridge.

Preparation time: 10 minutes
Cooking time: 0 Minutes (needs several hours in the refrigerator)
Serves: 20

Nutrition Facts Per Serving	
Calories	55
Protein	2 g
Cholesterol	0 mg
Fat	2 g
Carbohydrates	7 g
Fiber	Trace
Sodium	8 mg

Ingredients

- 1 pinch sea salt
- 12 1/3 ounces silken tofu, extra-firm or firm (do not use soft, medium or fresh tofu as icing won't be firm enough).
- 1/4 cup cashew, almond or hazelnut butter
- 1/4 cup brown rice syrup (or agave nectar)
- 1/4 cup light-colored granulated sugar
- 2 teaspoons ginger juice, fresh (squeezed from fresh, grated ginger root)
- 2 teaspoons lemon zest

Directions

1. Put all the ingredients in a food processor and blend them until the result is smooth.
2. Place it in a refrigerator uncovered for several hours and wait for the icing to firm.
3. Place it on a cooled cake (such as our recipe for Maple cake).
4. Serve the cake (you can refrigerate it for a little while, but not too long as the cake will become dry)

Special Tip

- Try different sweeteners like maple syrup, agave syrup, brown rice syrup, barley malt syrup or granulated sugar. You can also replace the lemon zest with lime zest.

78. Nirvana Nicoise Salad with Crispy Tofu and Mustard Vinaigrette

The thing that makes this salad great is that it's so easy to adapt it. Just add whatever vegetables you like. For example, you can make it with green beans, broccoli, carrots or even artichoke hearts. The key is to keep the vegetables crisp.

Preparation time: less than 20 minutes
Cooking time: 20 Minutes
Serves: 4

Nutrition Facts Per Serving	
Calories	593
Protein	26.6 g
Cholesterol	0 mg
Fat	11.8 g
Carbohydrates	103.5 g
Fiber	25.9 g
Sodium	505 mg

Ingredients

- 8 ounces of extra-firm organic tofu, drained
- 4 purple potatoes or any variety of fingerlings
- 16 asparagus spears
- 20 cherry tomatoes
- 1 cucumber, sliced
- 1 garlic clove, minced
- 1 shallot, minced
- 4 cups mixed greens

- 1 cup of snow peas (or green beans)
- 1/2 cup water
- 1/4 cup pitted olives
- 1/4 cup fresh chopped parsley
- 5 tablespoons apple cider vinegar (divided)
- 3 tablespoons Dijon mustard
- 3 tablespoons apple juice
- 2 tablespoons fresh chopped parsley
- 1 tablespoon olive oil
- 1 tablespoon maple syrup
- 1 tablespoon fresh thyme, chopped (divided)
- 1 teaspoon extra-virgin olive oil
- 1/2 teaspoon ground black pepper
- 1/4 teaspoon salt
- 3/4 teaspoon dried tarragon (divided)

Directions

1. To make the vinaigrette, gather 3 tablespoons of the apple cider vinegar, the olive oil, maple syrup, water, shallot, mustard, as well as the salt and black pepper in a food processor and process until smooth. Put the result in a bowl and add 1/2 teaspoon of tarragon, the parsley and thyme. Do the taste test and add seasoning to where you're happy with it.
2. For the crispy tofu, take a medium bowl and in it mix together 2 tablespoons of the apple cider vinegar, 1/2 a teaspoon of the tarragon, 1/2 a tablespoon of thyme, the garlic, and the apple juice and whisk it all. Next, slice the tofu into 1/2 inch slices and add them as well. Cover the bowl and let the tofu marinade for at least 30 minutes.
3. Take a medium non-stick pan, put in a teaspoon of oil and allow it to heat over a medium high heat. When ready, add the marinated tofu and give it 3-5 minutes per side – the idea is to sear the tofu closed, then set the tofu aside.
4. Take a pot, put in the potatoes and enough water to cover them, and bring the whole thing to a boil. You want the potatoes to become fork tender but still be firm. This will take about 15.
5. Take them from the heat, get rid of the water, let them cool and then peel and slice the potatoes into rounds. Add salt and pepper.

6. Cut the woody ends of the asparagus, then cut them into thirds and place them in a steamer over boiling water. Put the lid on and give them about 3 minutes. Be sure you don't overcook them! Remove the asparagus from the heat and set them aside.

7. In their place in the steamer go the snow peas. Again, put the lid on and give them about 1 minute. They should be bright green but still have snap to them.

8. In each plate begin with a bed of mixed greens, put on top the crispy tofu and arrange the potatoes, tomatoes, cucumbers, olives, asparagus and snow peas in a visually appealing manner. Sprinkle thyme and parsley over top, give it a drizzle of the mustard vinaigrette and serve.

79. Awesome Figs, Arugula Flatbread, Grapes and Balsamic Vinegar

Figs, arugula and grapes in balsamic vinegar; what a combination! Sweet, tart and bitter all come together in this dish to create something quite definitely special. Do make sure you can get fresh figs for this dish, as it will make all the difference, both in flavor and wholesomeness. After all, they're full of potassium and dietary fiber.

Preparation time: 15 minutes
Cooking time: 10 Minutes
Serves: 6

Nutrition Facts Per Serving	
Calories	341
Protein	7.5 g
Cholesterol	2 mg
Fat	5.5 g
Carbohydrates	66.8 g
Fiber	5.7 g
Sodium	428 mg

Ingredients

- Prepared pizza dough for 1 pizza (recipe below)
- Sprinkle of red pepper flakes
- Salt & ground black pepper to taste
- 14 grapes, halved
- 10 brown figs, halved
- Handful of arugula leaves

- 1 clove garlic, finely minced
- 1/2 onion, sliced
- 1/4 red onion sliced
- 3 tablespoons balsamic vinegar
- 2 teaspoons extra-virgin olive oil (divided)
- 1 teaspoon vegan butter

Directions

1. Put a pizza stone in the middle rack of your oven, then turn the oven to 500°F and let it preheat.
2. In the meantime, take a medium nonstick sauté pan and add 1 teaspoon of olive oil. When that's hot, sauté the onion, until they caramelize. Don't forget to stir. Then set them aside. Are the onions sticking to the pan? Use veggie stock rather than oil to avoid that.
3. Take a small pan and put it over a medium-low heat. Let the balsamic vinegar simmer until, until you've got about half the liquid left (about 3-4 teaspoons) and it's starting to get a syrupy consistency.
4. Wipe out the pan you used for the onion, put in the butter and let that come to a heat. Put the figs inside as a single layer and sear them closed quickly (It should take about 30 seconds). Put them aside as well.
5. Take your pizza dough (instructions are in the next recipe), stretch it to about 9 inches and sprinkle it with olive oil along with a bit of red pepper flakes.
6. Over top, sprinkle the minced garlic, then drizzle the thickened balsamic vinegar over top as well. Next the red onion and caramelized onions, then it's the turn of the figs, cut in two. Add a bit of seasoning with salt and pepper and you can put them in the oven. At this high of temperature it should only take about 5-10 minutes for the bread to rise and brown.
7. Scatter the arugula and the grapes over top and it is ready to be served.

80. Perfect Pizza Dough

With this recipe you won't just be able to bring pizza back into your life, but flat bread and other such recipes as well. What's more, this version, unlike what you buy in the store, doesn't have heaps of salt, fat or preservatives. Let's take pizza away from big business and put back in the wholesomeness that they've taken out!

Preparation time: 20 minutes
Cooking time: 10 minutes (needs to rise for about 40 minutes)
Serves: 8

Nutrition Facts Per Serving	
Calories	225
Protein	6 g
Cholesterol	0 mg
Fat	3 g
Carbohydrates	42.9 g
Fiber	1.8 g
Sodium	391 mg

Ingredients

- 1/4 ounce package of active dry yeast
- 2-2/12 cups white whole-wheat flour (or all-purpose flour)
- 3/4 cup cold water
- 1/4 cup warm water
- 2-4 tablespoons of cornmeal
- 1 tablespoon olive oil
- 1 teaspoon of maple syrup
- 1 teaspoons salt

Directions

1. Put a 1/4 cup of water into a bowl, add the yeast and wait for it to begin foaming after about 10 minutes. In a separate bowl combine cold water with the olive oil, salt and maple syrup.
2. In a separate bowl equipped with a dough hook, put 1 cup of flour, then mix in the yeast mixture. Continue to add flour and the water mixture alternatively as you combine, trying to keep the balance between the two. You're done when the dough is smooth and elastic and begins to form a ball and pull away from the bowl's sides.
3. Take it out of the mixture bowl and knead it for a few minutes more, then put it in a mixing bowl that you've oiled previously. Put a damp towel over the bowl and give it 30 minutes in a warm place to rise. The dough should approximately double in volume.
4. Put a pizza stone in the middle rack of your oven, then turn the oven to 500°F and let it preheat.
5. Spray a 19-inch pizza pan with olive oil. Then sprinkle the cornmeal across the surface.
6. Put the dough on a work surface that has a light layer of flour on it (to prevent sticking) and cut it into three balls. Knead these, and cover them with damp towels for 10 minutes.
7. Stretch the dough ball out into a pizza shape and put on your desired toppings. Put them in the oven and let it bake. It should take about 5 to 10 minutes, though your toppings might need longer. When the edges have browned the pizza is ready.

81. Glorious Glazed Donuts

These brilliant little balls of doughy goodness are a great alternative to the store-bought crap that you get out there, as here it's your recipe and you know exactly what goes in them. And they're terrific besides! Even our donut loving neighbors had to admit they weren't far off the 'real' thing.

Preparation time: 15 minutes
Cooking time: 15 Minutes
Serves: 3

Nutrition Facts Per Serving	
Calories	466
Protein	6 g
Cholesterol	44 mg
Fat	16.7 g
Carbohydrates	75.6 g
Fiber	1.4 g
Sodium	289 mg

Ingredients

- Egg replacer equivalent to one egg
- 1 cup all-purpose flour
- 1/2 cup organic sugar
- 1/2 cup and 1 tablespoon of non-dairy milk
- 1/2 cup confectioner's sugar
- 4 tablespoons Vegan Butter
- 1 1/2 teaspoon baking powder

- 1/2 teaspoon cinnamon (or nutmeg - experiment with spices you like)
- 1/2 teaspoon apple cider vinegar
- 1/2 teaspoon vanilla
- 1/4 teaspoon sea salt
- 3 or more tablespoon sprinkles (OPTIONAL)

Directions

1. Take a large bowl and put into it the flour, sugar, baking powder and cinnamon and whisk the resulting mixture well.
2. Place a small saucepan over a low heat and put 1/2 a cup of milk, the vinegar and the egg replacer into it. Follow the package instructions for the egg replacer. Also add the vegan butter and allow it to just melt. At this point you should still be able to touch the mixture and it should be warm rather than hot.
3. Take the wet ingredients off the fire, add them to the bowl with the dry ingredients and mix them to form a spongy batter.
4. This batter goes into a non-stick donut pan. Put it into an oven that's been preheated to 350°F. They'll need about 10-12 minutes. They'll be done when you stick in a toothpick comes out clean. Alternatively, use a donut maker and follow the maker's instructions.
5. Allow the donuts to cool on a cooling rack.
6. In the meantime make the glazing by mixing together the confectioner's sugar, 1 tablespoon of the milk and the vanilla. Dip the cooling donuts into this mixture to glaze them and then put them on a serving dish. Add sprinkles if you want.

82. Vibrant Vegetable and Tofu Stir Fry

Stir fries are quick, tasty and – because everything hasn't been overcooked – nutritious. This particular stir fry is high in vitamin A, B6 and C along with about two dozen other things. Mix and match your own choice of vegetables to get a different taste every time.

Preparation time: 10 minutes
Cooking time: 10 minutes
Serves: 2

Nutrition Facts Per Serving	
Calories	185
Protein	12.9 g
Cholesterol	0 mg
Fat	6.4 g
Carbohydrates	22.9 g
Fiber	4.9 g
Sodium	433 mg

Ingredients

- 8 ounces tofu, drained and cut in cubes
- 1 clove garlic, finely chopped
- 1 medium green onion, thinly sliced diagonally
- 1/2 carrot, peeled and sliced
- 1/2 red pepper, seeded and cut into strips
- 1/2 small head bok choy, chopped
- 1/4 medium onion, sliced
- 1 cup fresh mushrooms chopped

- 1/2 cup baby corn
- 1/2 cup bean sprouts
- 1/2 cup bamboo shoots, drained and chopped
- 1/4 cup water
- 2 tablespoon rice wine vinegar
- 1 tablespoon maple syrup
- 1 tablespoon soy sauce
- 1 1/2 teaspoon veg oil
- 1 1/2 teaspoon fresh ginger root finely chopped
- 1 teaspoon cornstarch dissolved in 1 tbsp water
- 1/4 teaspoon crushed red pepper

Directions

1. For this recipe, since you're not using oil or butter, you have to keep stirring throughout.
2. Put a large nonstick skillet over a medium heat, throw in the onions. After one minute, add garlic and the ginger and give wait 30 seconds. Put in the tofu and wait for it to become golden brown.
3. Add the carrots, corn and bell peppers. Wait for 2 more minutes and add the bok choy, bean sprouts, mushroom, bamboo shoots and crushed red pepper and wait for it to heat through, then take it from the fire.
4. Mix together the water, rice wine vinegar, maple syrup and soy sauce in a small pan. Allow it to cook for 2 minutes at a simmer. Then add the cornstarch to the water mixture. Wait for the sauce to thicken and pour it over the vegetables. Garnish with scallions and it is ready to be served.

83. Gratuitous Granola with Dark Chocolate and Cherries

In the stores they market granola bars as if they're a healthy choice. Take a look at their ingredients, however, and you'll find they're quite the opposite. They're often chock-full of salt, sugar and palm oils. Not these babies. These are as healthy as they're supposed to be. And you know what? They taste even better than the store-bought variety.

Preparation time: 10 minutes
Cooking time: 40 Minutes
Serves: 12 bars

Nutrition Facts Per Serving	
Calories	144
Protein	4.5 g
Cholesterol	0 mg
Fat	5.6 g
Carbohydrates	20.7 g
Fiber	2.7 g
Sodium	53 mg

Ingredients

- 1 1/2 cups old-fashioned rolled oats
- 3/4 cup slivered almonds
- 3/4 cup dried tart cherries
- 1/2 cup almond flour
- 1/2 cup wheat germ
- 1/2 cup apple sauce
- 1/3 cup maple syrup
- 1/3 cup vegan dark chocolate chips

- 1 teaspoon vanilla extract
- 1/2 teaspoon baking powder
- 1/4 teaspoon salt

Directions

1. Set the oven to 350°F and allow it to preheat.
2. Put the oats, wheat germ, flour, salt, baking powder, apple sauce, vanilla and maple syrup in a food processor and pulse until they've all been combined. Add the almonds, cherries and dark-chocolate chips.
3. Take a 9-inch square pan, line it with parchment paper and transfer the batter to it. Flatten it out to the desired thickness.
4. Put it in the oven and leave it for 40 minutes, until the edges begin to brown and if you press down on the center with your fingertip it is firm.
5. Take it out and let it cool. Using the parchment paper, lift the bar from the pan and place it onto a board. Cut into pieces (any size you prefer, though the nutritional information provided above was for 1 bar when it was cut into 12 pieces).
6. Enjoy.

84. Delightful Dates stuffed with Cashew Cream and Almonds

This plate of high protein goodness is a snap to prepare and a true pleasure to eat. The dates filled with cashew creams and almond milk create a wonderful combination of sweet and salty. Add to that that it's high in protein and low in salt and you can see the attraction. A (snack) party on a plate.

Preparation time: 5 minutes
Cooking time: 5
Serves: 4

Nutrition Facts Per Serving	
Calories	496
Protein	7.8 g
Cholesterol	0 mg
Fat	19.8 g
Carbohydrates	42.2 g
Fiber	8.5 g
Sodium	10 mg

Ingredients

- 2 cups of fresh dates
- 1 cup organic raw cashews (soaked for 2 hours or more)
- 1/4 cup almond milk (or more depending on desired thickness)
- 1 tablespoon maple syrup, or more to taste
- 1/4 teaspoon vanilla extract, or more to taste

Directions

1. Put all the ingredients except for the dates into a food processor and process until creamy. Add more almond milk if necessary.
2. Cut open the dates and spoon the filling into them.
3. Serve

85. Blessed Banana Bread and Walnuts

This recipe comes straight from a vegan chef, to your kitchen. It's a great dish to prepare beforehand and freeze. Then you can take them out when you need them for snacking purposes. Delicious, nutritious and easy, this really is the perfect way to fill that long gap between meals.

Preparation time: 15 minutes
Cooking time: 50 Minutes
Serves: 4

Nutrition Facts Per Serving	
Calories	542
Protein	24.8 g
Cholesterol	47 mg
Fat	13 g
Carbohydrates	72.5 g
Fiber	11.1 g
Sodium	353 mg

Ingredients

- 2 ripe bananas - sliced and then mashed
- 3/4 cup whole wheat pastry flour
- 1/2 cup plus 1 tablespoon coconut milk (or any unsweetened non-dairy milk)
- 1/2 cup maple syrup
- 1/2 cup walnuts, toasted, cooled and chopped
- 1/4 cup all-purpose flour
- 3 tablespoons olive oil
- 1 teaspoon baking powder

- 1 teaspoon cinnamon
- 1 teaspoon vanilla extract
- 1 teaspoon apple cider vinegar
- 1/2 teaspoon baking soda
- 1/4 teaspoon salt

Directions

1. Turn your oven to 375°F and allow it to preheat. Take a 8 1/2 x 4 1/2 loaf pan and apply oil.
2. Take the whole wheat flour, all-purpose flour, baking powder, cinnamon, baking soda and salt, pass them through a sieve and combine them all in a bowl.
3. Take the banana, coconut milk, maple syrup vanilla extra, apple cider vinegar and remaining olive oil and mix them together using a food processor.
4. Combine the two and stir until the result is smooth. Add the walnuts and stir (do NOT process, you want the walnuts to be chunky).
5. Add the mixture to the loaf pan and put them in the oven. Wait for about 50 minutes. At around this time if you put a toothpick in and it comes out clean, the banana bread is done.
6. Let it cool and you can serve it.

86. Creative Cashew Cheese, Tomato, Basil and Watercress

The vegan cheese in this dish isn't the easiest to make, but it is absolutely worth it. With it we've got this wonderful caprese dish, which is fresh, titillating and full of honest flavors, in the way only the Italian kitchen ever seems to be able to manage. So what am I saying? It's never the easy things you remember and this is a dish you won't soon forget.

Preparation time: 30 minutes
Cooking time: 0 minutes (needs 28 hours to culture)
Serves: 4

Nutrition Facts Per Serving	
Calories	403
Protein	25.3 g
Cholesterol	0 mg
Fat	44.8 g
Carbohydrates	89.3 g
Fiber	7.7 g
Sodium	1244 mg

Ingredients

- 2 French baguettes, split lengthwise and cut in half crosswise.
- 3-4 large roma tomatoes, sliced ¼ inch thick
- Sea Salt & Freshly ground black pepper
- Pinch of freshly grated nutmeg
- Fresh basil
- 1/2 teaspoon white pepper
- Basil oil for drizzling
- 2 cups whole raw cashews

- 1 cup watercress
- 2 tablespoons chopped fresh tarragon
- 2 tablespoons chopped fresh chives
- 2 tablespoons of olive oil
- 1 tablespoon of chopped basil
- 1 tablespoon nutritional yeast flakes
- 1 tablespoon onion powder
- 1 teaspoon probiotic
- 1 teaspoon sea salt

Directions

1. First, you need to make the cashew cheese. To do this, put the cashews in a bowl and put in enough cold water that they're covered. Put a lid on the bowl and refrigerate them for anywhere from 12 to 14 hours.
2. Combine 2 tablespoons of water with the probiotic powder mix it up until the resulting mixture is smooth. Put the nuts in a blender, along with the mixture you just made and blend the result on high for several minutes. Stop every little bit of time to scrape the nuts off the side, so that no chunks are left over. You want the mixture to be smooth.
3. Take a sieve and apply three layers of rinsed and squeezed cheesecloth to the inside, making sure there's plenty of overhang over the edges. Set this into a bowl then take the mixture from the blender and pour it inside. Take the excess cheesecloth, collect it together, seal it and squeeze the mixture down through the cheesecloth and the sieve.
4. Put some heavy objects onto the cloth (cans will work) and leave it in a warm place for 14 to 16 hours. This will allow the cheese to culture.
5. Afterward, put the cheese in a medium bowl.
6. Add the onion powder, nutritional yeast, white pepper, nutmeg and salt, while mixing. When it's all mixed together, take a sheet of parchment paper and scoop the mixture into the middle of it. Carefully, roll the paper so that you ve got a 2-inch diameter log. This goes into the refrigerator for at least several hours but preferably overnight. It will turn firm.
7. Spread the herbs and pepper onto a tray, take the log, unwrap it and then roll it in the mixture of herbs, so that the surface is coated. Cut the log into thin slices, about 1/4 of an inch across.

8. Take our baguettes, slice them in half and put your watercress on the bottom half. Take the basil oil and drizzle it over the cress, then add tomato, season it with salt and pepper, and finally add a slice of the cheese. Put the other half of the baguette on top and serve immediately (otherwise you'll lose the baguette's crispiness).

87. Awesome Asian Rice Noodle Salad with Tofu

This spicy tofu noodle salad with vagrant spices is a taste of the orient in your home. It really is quite wonderful, with its jalapeno based spiciness, its soy sauce saltiness and its limey freshness. Your family will eat every last noodle, hunt down ever last almond sliver and beg you to make more.

Preparation time: 20 minutes
Cooking time: 10 Minutes
Serves: 2-4

Nutrition Facts Per Serving	
Calories	193
Protein	8.7 g
Cholesterol	0 mg
Fat	3.5 g
Carbohydrates	34 g
Fiber	2.7 g
Sodium	363 mg

Ingredients

- 1 8 ounce packaged tofu, cut into small cubes
- 1 Thai chili or jalapeno, seeded and thinly sliced (more if you like spicy)
- 3 cloves garlic, minced (1 tablespoon)
- 5 oz. dried rice noodles
- 6 scallions sliced thin - white part only
- 1 1/2 cups thinly sliced purple cabbage or radicchio
- 1 1/2 cups julienned cucumbers
- 1 cup chopped fresh basil

- 1/2 cup almond slivers
- 1/2 cup lime juice
- 1/4 cup cornstarch
- 1/4 cup additional low-sodium soy to marinate tofu
- 3 tablespoon low-sodium soy sauce
- 3 1/2 teaspoon dark brown sugar

Directions

1. Put the tofu and a 1/4 cup of soy sauce in a bowl and let it marinate.
2. In a small bowl, combine the brown sugar, soy sauce, chile and garlic and whisk until the sugar is dissolved.
3. In a larger bowl combine the cucumber, basil, green onion and cabbage. Add some of the lime mixture and toss well.
4. Take the tofu from the marinade and toss it with the cornstarch, then add it to a nonstick skillet and sauté it over a medium-high heat until the tofu has browned. Add in the cabbage mixture and toss them through each other. You might want to add more lime.
5. Cook the noodles according to the instructions on the package.
6. Divide the noodles across the plates, then put the tofu mixture on top and sprinkle the almonds across the plates. It is ready to be served.

88. Beautiful Baby Jackfruit Barbeque Sandwich

Jackfruit is an Asian fruit that due to its meaty texture is a great meat substitute. Just adding it to this dish gives this sandwich that real deal feel. Do be careful about what jackfruit you actually buy, however. You want the green kind as the other kind won't taste half as good.

Preparation time: less than 5 minutes
Cooking time: 1 hour 15 Minutes (also needs a night in the refrigerator)
Serves: 2

Nutrition Facts Per Serving	
Calories	309
Protein	1.6 g
Cholesterol	0 mg
Fat	06 g
Carbohydrates	77.9 g
Fiber	2.8 g
Sodium	1308 mg

Ingredients

- 4 cloves garlic, minced
- 15 ounce can green jackfruit (In brine or water) drained and rinsed well, squeezed of extra water
- A couple of pinches of ground chipotle pepper
- 1/2 cup of your favorite barbecue sauce
- 1/4 cup water
- 1/4 cup veggie broth
- 2 teaspoon grated ginger root

- 1/2 teaspoon liquid smoke
- 1/2 teaspoon salt

Directions

1. Place a nonstick skillet over a medium heat.
2. Put the vegie broth, garlic and ginger into the pan and let them sauté for 1-2 minutes until the liquid has evaporated.
3. Now add in the jackfruit, liquid smoke, chipotle and salt and while stirring cook it for another 4-5 minutes.
4. The mixture next goes into the slow cooker, along with the barbeque sauce and the water. Make sure everything is mixed well.
5. Set the cooker to 'HIGH' and let it run for 1 hour, stirring every 15 minutes or so and adding water as needed. You're looking for the jack fruit to become fork tender.
6. Take the jackfruit out and with two forks shred it.
7. Put it in a Tupperware box and give it a night in the refrigerator. Then reheat it when you want to serve.
8. It goes well with coleslaw.

89. Brazenly Broccoli Soup with Toasted Croutons

Broccoli is an amazing vegetable that is so chock full of nutrients when you put it into a dish with other vegetables, they actually feel embarrassed. No really, go on and ask them. Nobody will think you're weird. This goodness bomb is a great way to load up on the nutrients. Oh and if you want to put in more protein, try exchanging the bread croutons for nuts.

Preparation time: 10 minutes
Cooking time: 15 minutes
Serves: 4

Nutrition Facts Per Serving	
Calories	85
Protein	8.4 g
Cholesterol	0 mg
Fat	1.8 g
Carbohydrates	10.1 g
Fiber	3.4 g
Sodium	1117 mg

Ingredients

- 1 pound broccoli, separated into florets
- 4 cups and 2 tablespoons vegetable broth
- 1/2 cup chopped onions
- 2 tablespoons chopped fresh parsley
- 2 teaspoons of dried basil
- 1/2 teaspoon salt (or to taste)
- 1/2 teaspoon fresh ground black pepper

Directions

1. Preheat the oven to 400°F
2. Take the broccoli and chop it up coarsely.
3. Put 2 tablespoons of the vegetable broth into a saucepan and put it on a medium heat. Add the dried basil and onions, then give it about 5 minutes to cook, while stirring. Wait for the onions to turn translucent. If the onions are sticking to the pan, don't be afraid to add a little bit more vegetable broth.
4. Add the 4 cups of vegetable broth along with the broccoli and turn the heat up to high, till it boils. Then reduce the temperature down till it's simmering. You want the broccoli to be fork tender. This will take about 10 minutes.
5. In the meantime, chop up some vegan bread into bite sized chunks, add a teaspoon of olive oil and parsley, spread them out over a baking sheet in a single layer and pop them in the oven for about 5-10 minutes.
6. Put the content of the sauce pan into a blender and blend until it is smooth. Now add the parsley, salt and pepper. Hit the pulse button a few times, then put the soup back in the pan and reheat it gently, while adding seasoning.
7. Scoop into plates, top with golden croutons and serve.

90. Blissful Brussel Sprouts and Chestnut Mustard Sauce

This is a beautiful holiday season dish, with the strong flavor of the Brussel sprouts balanced by the crunchy fullness of the chestnuts and the zest of the lemon-mustard dressing. If you want a bit more bite, consider replacing the grainy mustard with horse radish.

Preparation time: 15 minutes
Cooking time: 30 minutes
Serves: 8

Nutrition Facts Per Serving	
Calories	360
Protein	3.5 g
Cholesterol	0 mg
Fat	31 g
Carbohydrates	20.7 g
Fiber	3.4 g
Sodium	461 mg

Ingredients

- 20 ounces fresh Brussels Sprouts, trimmed
- 8 tablespoons vegan butter (use less if you want) You can also replace some of it with vegie broth
- 1/2 pound fresh chestnuts
- 2 lemons, juiced
- 3/4 cup extra-virgin olive oil (start with 1/2 cup and add more if needed)
- 3 tablespoons Dijon mustard
- 2 teaspoons fresh thyme leaves, chopped

- 1 teaspoon whole grain mustard
- 1 teaspoon salt
- 1/2 teaspoon freshly ground pepper

Directions

1. Cut two groves in the shape of an X into the flat side of each chestnut shell, put them in a saucepan, cover them with water and bring them to boil. Reduce heat and let them simmer until they are tender, which will take about 15 minutes. Drain off the water and when the chestnuts are cool enough to handle without getting burned, peel them.
2. Put a large pot on the fire, add salt and let it come to a boil. Put in the cleaned Brussel sprouts and cook them until they are tender, but still a tiny bit firm. This should take about 5-6 minutes. Drain of the water and run the Brussel sprouts under cold water.
3. Put the butter in a large skillet and melt it over a medium heat. That done, add in the peeled chestnuts and the Brussel sprouts. Add a bit of salt and pepper seasoning and cook them until they are browned. This will take about 10 to 15 minutes. Make sure you turn them over occasionally.
4. Using a slotted spoon, take out the vegetables and put them on a serving platter.
5. Make the dressing by taking the lemon juice, both mustards, olive oil, salt, thyme and pepper and whisking it together. When adding it to the vegetables do so slowly as it has a strong taste and too much will ruin the dish. You'll need about a 1/4 cup.
6. It is ready to be served.

91. Corn & Magical Mushroom Pasta Frittatas

This pasta frittata is just a beautiful family dinner and it's versatile as well. You can easily replace the vegetables mentioned here with what you prefer, like peas or chopped spinach. It goes especially well with a salad on the side. Before you serve this dish, your dinner companions might not know what a Frittata is, afterwards they'll want to know how they can get more.

Preparation time: 10 minutes
Cooking time: 30 Minutes
Serves: 4

Nutrition Facts Per Serving	
Calories	334
Protein	23.8 g
Cholesterol	23 mg
Fat	8.8 g
Carbohydrates	45.7 g
Fiber	4.9 g
Sodium	1132 mg

Ingredients

- Fresh ground black pepper
- 3 cups sliced mushrooms (approximately 8-9 ounces)
- 2 1/2 cups of drained extra firm tofu
- 1 1/2 cups fresh organic corn kernels (about 2 ears) – frozen corn works as well
- 1 cup cooked whole-wheat angel hair pasta
- 1/2 cup fresh chopped basil (and a handful for garnish)
- 1/2 cup dry breadcrumbs (and some for sprinkling on top)

- 1/3 cup green onions, chopped
- 3 tablespoons of soy sauce
- 2 tablespoons of vegetable broth
- 1 tablespoon nutritional yeast
- 1/4 teaspoon black pepper
- 1/4 teaspoon hot sauce (like tabasco)
- 1/2 teaspoon salt

Directions

1. Turn your oven up to 375°F and allow it to preheat
2. Take a food processor and put into it the tofu, nutritional yeast, hot sauce, black pepper and soy sauce, then process it until the mixture is creamy and thick. Add in the breadcrumbs, stir it up and set it aside.
3. Take an oven safe sate pan (if you don't have one, then transfer the mixture to a baking dish or pie pan when you need to put it in the oven). Put in the vegetable broth and place it on a medium-high heat. Sauté the green onions, mushrooms, and corn until they turn soft.
4. Combine in the cooked pasta, then stir in the tofu mixture as well as the basil until it is well blended.
5. Take it off the heat, add the bread crumbs. And put it in the oven for 20 minutes, so that it has browned at the top and is firm all over. Sprinkle the extra green onion and the fresh basil over top and it is ready to be served.

92. Heavenly Hummus & Hemp Seed Pita Pockets

This traditional little dish with a modern twist is a combination of nuttiness and zest that will have almost anybody humming a tune (or is that just me who does that with delicious food?). Add to that that hemp, with all 10 essential amino acids, is going to have your engine humming along and you can see why sometimes classical recipes have to make a comeback.

Preparation time: 10 minutes
Cooking time: 5 minutes
Serves: 2

Nutrition Facts Per Serving	
Calories	747
Protein	38.5 g
Cholesterol	0 mg
Fat	17.2 g
Carbohydrates	115.3 g
Fiber	30.5 g
Sodium	300 mg

Ingredients

- Salt and ground black pepper
- 1 whole-wheat pita
- 1 1/2 cups cooked chickpeas
- 1/2 cup cucumber, diced
- 1/2 cup tomatoes, diced
- 1/2 cup water
- 1/4 cup red pepper, diced

- 1/4 cup parsley, chopped
- 4 tablespoons hemp seeds
- 2 tablespoons green onion (or shallots)
- 2 tablespoons lemon juice
- 2 tablespoons lemon juice
- 2 teaspoons garlic

Directions

1. In a saucepan, bring 1/2 a cup of water to a boil. Then add the cooked chickpeas, garlic and give it one minute. Take it from the heat and mash the result coarsely. Stir in the hemp seeds, lemon juice and then season with both salt and pepper.
2. Take a small bowl, put into it the tomato, red pepper, parsley, cucumber, lemon juice and green onion and mix them together. If you want, add salt and pepper.
3. Each pitta half gets 1/3 cup of hummus and 1/2 a cup of the cucumber salad.

93. Quality Cheese and Broccoli Quiche

There's a good reason why they serve quiche at almost every coffee place and café in the country. It's easy to make, tasty and stays good for long indeed. All that is equally true of this quiche, but it has a further advantage in that because it's home made you decide on what goes into it, like much less salt ,which makes it better than anything store bought, let me tell you!

Preparation time: 20 minutes
Cooking time: 1 hour
Serves: 4

Nutrition Facts Per Serving	
Calories	473
Protein	17 g
Cholesterol	0 mg
Fat	20.5 g
Carbohydrates	62.5 g
Fiber	10.2 g
Sodium	1397 mg

Ingredients

- 7 ounces silken tofu
- 7 ounces broccoli, broken into florets
- 5 ounces plain flour
- 2 ounces vegan margarine
- 2 ounces of Vegusto Classic cheese, grated
- 1 small onion, chopped
- 1 clove garlic, crushed

- 4 large sundried tomatoes, sliced
- Salt and pepper
- 1 1/4 cup water
- 1 tablespoon olive oil
- 4 teaspoon The Vegg

Directions

1. Set your oven to 400°F and allow it to preheat.
2. First make the pastry. To do this, take a mixing bowl and sieve the flour into it. Then rub in the vegan margarine and salt.
3. Slowly add the water, while mixing the soon-to-be dough with a spoon. Push down on the dough with your fist to make sure all the flour has been incorporated into it.
4. Apply flour to a rolling pin and then use it to roll out the dough into a large thin circle.
5. Grease a 10 inch pop-bottom flan dish. Take the flattened dough and put it inside.
6. Press it into the shape of the flan dish and trim any that comes over the side away.
7. Let it bake for 5 minutes in the oven. Set it aside.
8. In the meantime, put the broccoli in a steamer (or boil it) for a few minutes. The aim is to have it keep its crunch.
9. Take The Vegg and mix it together with water in a mixing bowl. Then add the silken tofu, mix again. Add salt and pepper to taste.
10. In a nonstick skillet fry up the onions and garlic until they've turned soft. This should take about 5 minutes.
11. Time to assemble the quiche. First arrange the broccoli, onion and garlic in the pastry case. Next, add the tofu/vegg mix over the top. Make sure it mixes well. Over top apply the Vegusto Classic cheese, as well as the sun-dried tomatoes. Season it with salt and pepper.
12. It will need 45 minutes in the oven. You're looking for the content to have cooked and the filling to have set. You can test it by pushing a knife into the center, to check for firmness.
13. You can serve the dish hot or cold. It works well with a nice salad.

94. Surreal Shepard's Pie

Shepard's pie is such a fantastic winter recipe that to go your whole life without it would be a life not lived. For that reason we've adapted it to the vegan kitchen, using a great mince substitute, so that we too can feel all warm and cozy on the inside when the wind is whipping at the branches outside.

Preparation time: 20 minutes
Cooking time: 45 minutes
Serves: 8

Nutrition Facts Per Serving	
Calories	439
Protein	24.7 g
Cholesterol	0 mg
Fat	11.2 g
Carbohydrates	61.4 g
Fiber	20.6 g
Sodium	296 mg

Ingredients

- Salt and ground black pepper
- 35 ounces potatoes, peeled, cut into pieces
- 14 ounce can cannellini beans, drained and rinsed
- 14 ounce can diced tomatoes
- 10 ounces Vegideli Mince
- 1 onion, finely chopped
- 1 clove of garlic, crushed
- 1 large carrot chopped finely

- 1 leek thinly sliced
- 1/2 cup of soy milk
- Salt and freshly ground black pepper
- 3 Tablespoon tomato purée
- 2 tablespoon vegan margarine
- 1 tablespoon oil
- 2 teaspoon of chopped fresh or dried thyme leaves
- 1 heaped teaspoon sugar

Directions

1. Turn the oven to 375°F and let it preheat.
2. To make the topping, put the potatoes into a large pan and add water. Let it come to a boil and let it go for 12-15 minutes, until the potatoes are tender. Drain off the water.
3. Add the margarine to the potatoes and mash them up well. Then it's time to add the soy milk a dash at a time, while you continue mashing until the texture is smooth. Add a little bit of salt and pepper and put it aside.
4. For the filling, take a large nonstick skillet and in it heat oil over a medium heat. Add in the onion and let it sauté for 8-10 minutes until the onions have softened. Don't forget to stir.
5. Next, add in carrot, leek garlic and thyme and let it go for another 4-5 minutes and the vegetables have softened.
6. Put in the Vegideli mince and while stirring let it go for 2-3 minutes. You want the meat substitute to become golden brown.
7. Now it is time to add in the cannellini beans, chopped tomatoes and tomato purée. Stir the mixture well until everything has combined nicely. Let the mixture simmer for 4-5 minutes, or until the sauce has thickened. Add a bit of salt and pepper and perhaps some sugar, if it is needed.
8. Take a large ovenproof dish and spoon the filling into it, then spread the mashed potato overtop in an even layer.
9. Put the dish in the oven and let it cook for 18-20 minutes. You want the topping is to turn golden-brown and the filling to be cooked all the way through.
10. It is ready to be served

95. Lovely Lemongrass Consommé with Tofu Dumplings

This surprisingly easy dish is just scrumptious. It is a wonderful alternative to the norm, with its zesty consommé and succulent tofu mushroom dumplings. You might just want to keep it for special occasions, or you might just want to use it to make one day a week special. With this recipe it's all up to you.

Preparation time: 20 minutes
Cooking time: 55 Minutes
Serves: 4

Nutrition Facts Per Serving	
Calories	505
Protein	15.9 g
Cholesterol	0 mg
Fat	16.6 g
Carbohydrates	75.3 g
Fiber	4.8 g
Sodium	865 mg

Ingredients

- 12 round wonton skins
- 6 basil leaves, chopped
- 4 stalks lemongrass
- 3 cloves garlic, peeled and smashed
- 2-4 ounces firm tofu
- 2 quarts vegetable stock
- 2 stalks celery, diced
- 2 shallots, minced

- 2 small dried red chiles
- 1 leek, thinly sliced
- 1 (2-inch) piece fresh ginger, peeled and diced
- 3/4 pound mushrooms, minced
- 1/2 lime zest
- Freshly ground black pepper to taste
- Sea salt
- 4 tablespoons canola or vegetable oil (divided)
- 2 tablespoons sugar
- 1 tablespoon fresh parsley, minced
- 2 teaspoons of fresh ginger
- 2 teaspoons soy sauce
- 1 1/2 teaspoon finely chopped chives
- 1 teaspoon whole black peppercorns
- 2 small Bok Choy, chopped (OPTIONAL)

Directions

1. Start by making the consommé by placing a large stockpot over medium heat and adding a pinch of salt to it. Then put in 2 tablespoons of oil. When it is hot, put in the vegetable oil, lemongrass, celery, leek, shallots, ginger, lime zest, red chiles and peppercorns. Let it all sauté for 5 minutes as you stir frequently.
2. Then add the sugar and the stock as well and let it come to a boil, reduce the heat and let it simmer for 45 minutes.
3. In the meantime, to make the dumplings, take a medium nonstick skillet and place it over a medium heat. Add a bit of salt, let it heat for one minute, then add in the oil and let it get hot (but not so hot it smokes). Put in the mushrooms and sauté them for 2 to 3 minutes, while you occasionally stir, until they've let their fluid go. Now put in the chives, basil, ginger, tofu and soy sauce and add a bit of salt and pepper as well, to create the right taste. Let it sauté for another 1 minute. You're looking for all the ingredients to have mixed and become tender. Now, transfer to a bowl and let it cool.
4. Clear a work surface and make sure it's dry and clean. Lay the wonton wraps, along with your ingredients and a bowl of water. Put a spoon full of filling in the center, wet your fingertips and dab the edge of the wonton with water, so that it becomes sticky. Fold the wonton over into a half-moon and scrunch and crimp the edges together.

5. Take a sieve and pour through it the consommé. Get rid of the solid and return the liquid to the pot. Let it come to a simmer, add in the dumplings (and the optional boy choy) and give it 10 minutes to simmer.
6. Garnish it with bits of sliced scallion and serve.

96. Wicked Roasted Pear with Ginger and Walnut

Be warned, this brilliant simple little starter will raise expectations of your culinary arts sky high, as people will come from far and wide to try your recipes. Here the combination of the roasted pears and the ginger really make the dish work, give this sweet crunchy recipe just that bit of bite it needs.

Preparation time: 15 minutes
Cooking time: 30 minutes
Serves: 4

Nutrition Facts Per Serving	
Calories	162
Protein	1.9 g
Cholesterol	0 mg
Fat	5.4 g
Carbohydrates	23.9 g
Fiber	6 g
Sodium	359 mg

Ingredients

- 5 comice pears
- 2 1/2 ounces walnut halves
- 1 ounce pine nuts
- 1 1/2 teaspoon ground cinnamon
- 1 teaspoon caraway seeds
- 1 ounce stem ginger (OPTIONAL)

Directions

1. Turn you oven to 350°F and let it preheat. In the meantime, halve and core all but one of the pears, take an ovenproof dish and place them inside flesh side up. Over top sprinkle the caraway seeds, as well as 1/2 a teaspoon of cinnamon.
2. Put them in the oven for 20-25 minutes. You want to edges to be browning and the flesh to be turning soft. Take them out and let them cool.
3. Take a baking tray and spread the pine nuts and walnuts out on the bottom. Put them in the oven for 4-5 minutes. Be careful with the pine nuts, they will be ready quickly.   Set   this   aside   as   well. Take the cooled pears, take out most of the flesh of four of them (but not so much they collapse). The rest you chop up. Put the chopped up pears and the flesh it all in the food processor, along with the toasted nut. Also add the ginger and the 1 teaspoon of cinnamon and blend the result. You don't want to make it totally smooth. Instead you're looking for a paste-like substance.
4. Divide the mixture out between the pear skins, filling them u. Take the one pear you have left over and slice it into thin slices. Put these on top of your stuffed pears along with a sprinkle of toasted pine nuts as garnish.
5. It is ready to be served. They work cold as well.

97. Awesome Asparagus Quinoa Risotto

It doesn't matter that it is winter and that it's the middle of the night, when you build this beauty, you're bringing a bit of sunshine into your home. Delicious, filling and oh so very summery Mediterranean style, this one is like a dawn at your dinner table.

Preparation time: 15 minutes
Cooking time: 25 Minutes
Serves: 2

Nutrition Facts Per Serving	
Calories	396
Protein	13 g
Cholesterol	0 mg
Fat	10 g
Carbohydrates	73 g
Fiber	11 g
Sodium	501 mg

Ingredients

1. 1 pound shiitake mushrooms, sliced
2. 2 medium leeks, chopped (use all)
3. 2 pounds asparagus, in 1/2" long pieces
4. 3 1/3 cups no-salt-added mushroom broth (or water) (divided)
5. 1 1/2 cups quinoa, washed
6. 1/3 cup tahini
7. 1 1/2 tablespoon olive oil
8. 2 teaspoon sea salt (divided)
9. 1/2 teaspoon Espelette powder

Directions

1. Wash the quinoa, then put it in a sauce pan along with 3 cups of mushroom broth, 1 teaspoon of the oil and 1/2 a teaspoon of sea salt. Put the lid on it and let it come to a boil. Then turn it down and let it simmer for 20-25 minutes.

2. In the meantime, put a pan on a medium high heat and put the 1/2 tablespoon of oil in it. That done, throw in the mushroom and let them sauté until the moisture has cooked off and they have started to brown a little. Throw the leek in as well and give it 5 more minutes. Add the asparagus. This time only cook until they're barely tender. Add the 1/2 teaspoon of sea salt, leave it on the fire for 1 minute longer.

3. Combine the tahini, 1/2 a cup of mushroom broth, tea spoon of sea salt and espelette powder in a bowl and combine. Then add it to the vegetables and mix again. Finally, the vegetables go in with the quinoa. Mix one more time and serve.

98. African Saffron Stew

It's something to do with the saffron I think, but whatever it is this Moroccan-inspired dish is a lovely combination of spices that will transport you straight to the Mediterranean coast. In this dish there's a hint of that fantastic Moroccan cooking method the tajine, but without you actually needing one of those large clay devices.

Preparation time: 20 minutes
Cooking time: 40 Minutes
Serves: 8

Nutrition Facts Per Serving	
Calories	322
Protein	11 g
Cholesterol	0 mg
Fat	6 g
Carbohydrates	61 g
Fiber	9 g
Sodium	716 mg

Ingredients

- 4 medium carrots, cut in half moons
- 3 cups butternut squash, peeled and cubed
- 2 medium onions, chopped
- 2 large plantains, peeled
- 1 bunch cilantro, chopped
- 28 ounces canned diced tomatoes
- 2 1/2 cups vegetable broth, no-salt-added (or water)
- 2 1/2 cups garbanzo beans, cooked, rinsed, drained

- 3 teaspoons olive oil (divided)
- 1 teaspoon turmeric
- 3/4 teaspoon sea salt (divided)
- 1/2 teaspoon ground ginger
- 1/2 teaspoon saffron threads, crushed

Directions

1. To make the winter squash, take a bowl and put into it the butternut squash cubes, a 1/4 teaspoon of salt, and 1 teaspoon of olive oil. Cover a baking sheet with parchment papers and transfer the content of the boil onto the parchment, spreading it into a single layer.
2. Turn your oven to 350°F and let the squash roast for about 30 minutes. You want it to turn soft and become slightly caramelized. Be sure to toss the vegetables a few time in the second half of the roast as otherwise they'll burn.
3. In the meantime, cut the plantains lengthwise and then turn them into 1/2 inch thick half moons by slicing them up. In a bowl, add the plantains along with 1 teaspoon of olive oil and a 1/4 teaspoon of salt then toss it all.
4. Take another baking tray, add a parchment sheet to it and spread out the plantains in a single layer.
5. Add them to the same oven. They will need about 15 minutes to roast, at which point they should be lightly browned.
6. It is possible that the plantains won't cook fully this way. In that case, put them in a pan add the broth to it and bring it to boil, then turn the heat down and let it simmer until the plantains have become soft. This could take up to 20 minutes. Be sure to add more liquid if it all boils off.
7. As the vegetables roast, you need to make the stew. For that take a pot and put it over a medium to high heat. Add in 1 teaspoon of olive oil and when that is hot, put in the onions. Give them about 10 minutes. Next, put in the carrots and give it another 15 minutes. Then, with the turmeric and ginger, let it cook 2 minutes more.
8. Put in the diced tomatoes, the saffron, a 1/4 teaspoon of sea salt and the garbanzo beans. Let it come to a simmer, then add in both the butternut squash and the stewed plantains. It needs another 5 minutes. If it is too thick add water.
9. Finally, garnish with the cilantro.

99. Brilliant Indian Biriyani

As India is in many ways the home of vegetarianism we'd be doing something close to criminal if we wouldn't at least include this wonderful biriyani dish. Use it as flavorsome replacement for ordinary rice, or have it on its own with a nice salad. And be sure to tell everybody what it's called, because 'biriyani' is just a really great word.

Preparation time: 15 minutes
Cooking time: 30 Minutes
Serves: 3

Nutrition Facts Per Serving	
Calories	424
Protein	14 g
Cholesterol	0 mg
Fat	13 g
Carbohydrates	60 g
Fiber	7 g
Sodium	200 mg

Ingredients

- 15 ounces basmati rice
- 4 ounces red lentils
- 4 ounces French bean, trimmed and cut in half
- 2 ounces roasted cashew nuts, roughly chopped
- 5 garlic cloves
- 2 potato cut into chunks
- 2 handfuls frozen pea
- 1 cauliflower cut into florets

- 1 large onion, roughly chopped
- 1 small green chilli
- Handful curry leaves
- Small bunch coriander
- Large piece ginger, roughly chopped
- Poppadoms and naan bread, to serve
- 2 tablespoons vegetable oil
- 2 tablespoons vegetable oil
- 2 teaspoons curry powder
- 1 teaspoon cumin
- Pinch saffron threads (OPTIONAL)

Directions

1. Let the rice soak for 30 mins. Rinse it well and several times to really get it to be clean. Put it in a pan, add enough water so it's about 1/2 an inch under water and add the saffron.
2. Let the rice come to a boil, stir it once vigorously, then put the lid on it. Let it cook for 10 minutes, stir it one more time, then take it off the heat and leave it to stand, with the lid on.
3. It's time to make the paste. Put the onion, ginger, garlic, curry powder, cumin, and chilli in a food processor and process them until the mixture is fine. Put 2 tablespoons of vegetable oil in a saucepan, let it heat over a medium to high heat then add the paste. Let the paste cook until the color shifts. Then add the lentils and the green beans. Also add another 14 ounces of water.
4. Put the curry leaves into the pot and season with salt. Put the lid on and let it simmer for about 20 minutes. You want the lentils and the vegetables to have turned tender. Then put in the peas for the last 2 minutes so they can defrost.
5. Take the rice, drain it of any leftover water and then stir it through the curry until well mixed. Divided it over the plates, add the coriander and the cashews and it is ready to be served.

100. Boisterous Tempeh Bourguignon

This stew is based on the beef bourguignon as served in French, but then (obviously) without the beef. In truth, it really doesn't need it, for the bourguignon is full of flavor all on its own through the use of wine and other wonderful additions. Do note that the better the wine, the better the flavor.

Preparation time: 20 minutes
Cooking time: 40 minutes
Serves: 4

Nutrition Facts Per Serving	
Calories	387
Protein	19 g
Cholesterol	0 mg
Fat	12 g
Carbohydrates	39 g
Fiber	5 g
Sodium	629 mg

Ingredients

- 16 ounces tempeh, defrosted
- 12 garlic cloves, minced (divided)
- 5 carrots, diced
- 2 large onions, diced
- 1 bay leaf
- 2 1/2 cups red wine (divided)
- 1 1/2 cups no-salt-added vegetable broth (or water)
- 1 cup peas, frozen

- 1/4 cup brown rice flour (or spelt flour)
- 2 tablespoons unrefined granulated sugar
- 1 tablespoon Tamari soy sauce
- 1 tablespoon dark miso
- 3/4 teaspoon sea salt (divided)
- 1/2 teaspoon ground thyme
- 1/4 teaspoon ground black pepper

Directions

1. To prepare the tempeh, cut it into cubes and place it in a 9x9 baking pan. Add in 1 1/2 cup of wine, 2 tablespoons of olive oil, sugar, 4 cloves of garlic, 1/2 teaspoon of sea salt and miso in a saucepan and heat it on a medium to high heat to get it up to cooking. When it does, pour it over the tempeh. Place the baking pan in a preheated oven that is at 450°F and let it go for about 35 minutes. It is ready when all the liquid has been absorbed.
2. While the tempeh is in the oven, take a large pot and put it over a medium-high heat. Put in 1 1/2 tablespoons of oil, then when that's hot sauté the onions for 7 minutes, then add the carrots wait for another 6 minutes and put in the 4 cloves of garlic for 2 minutes.
3. When all of these have been sealed, add in the flour and the thyme. Add the flower slowly and give it 2 more minutes. Next the tempeh goes in, along with the peas, bay leaf, 1 cup of wine, broth, 1/4 teaspoon of sea salt, and black pepper. Let all of this simmer for 10 minutes. You want to sauce to thicken.
4. Take out the bay leaf, mix in the tamari and it is ready to be served.

101. Tremendous Thai Basil Coconut Soup

This Thai soup does that thing with lemongrass that only Thai food can and in the process makes it creamy, zingy, fragrant and refreshing. It's always amazing how they can do that, isn't it?

Preparation time: 10 minutes
Cooking time: 30 minutes
Serves: 8

Nutrition Facts Per Serving	
Calories	161
Protein	3 g
Cholesterol	0 mg
Fat	12 g
Carbohydrates	13 g
Fiber	3 g
Sodium	239 mg

Ingredients

- 14 ounces coconut milk
- 4 garlic cloves, minced
- 3 medium carrots, sliced thin
- 1 small leek, sliced thin
- 1 stalk fresh lemon grass, finely minced (white part only - use rest for the broth)
- 1 medium red bell pepper, cubed
- 1/2 pound mushrooms, quartered (about 2 cups when cut)
- 2 1/4 cups kombu-ginger broth
- 3/4 cup green onions, chopped fine (about 6 stalks)

- 1/4 cup fresh basil, chopped
- 4 tablespoons cilantro, chopped fine
- 1 tablespoon unrefined granulated sugar
- 1 tablespoon white miso
- 1/2 teaspoon sea salt
- 1/4 teaspoon dark (toasted) sesame oil
- 1/8 teaspoon red chili flakes

Directions

1. Take a large pot and put in the oil and put it over a medium-high heat. Then stir frequently as you add the vegetables. Begin with Sautéing the mushrooms until they've lost their moisture. Next add the leek and sauté for 6 minutes. The carrots go in next and they also need 6 minutes.
2. Put in the bell pepper and wait another 5 minutes. Then put in the garlic and the white part of the lemon grass. It needs 3 more minutes now.
3. Next, put in the coconut milk, broth and the salt. Once all of this is cooking, turn down the heat to where it's only just simmering. Give it 5 more minutes.
4. Before you serve it, stir in the miso, making sure it's dissolved. Add the basil over top and sprinkle a bit of green onions and cilantro over top. It is ready to be served.

One Last Thing…

If you enjoyed this book or found it useful I'd be very grateful if you left a review. Your support makes all the difference and I read all of your reviews personally so I can get feedback to make this book (and my future books) even better.

For free eBooks go to

TimothyPyke.com

38803459R00129

Printed in Great Britain
by Amazon